Chemistry
ADDISON-WESLEY

Guided Reading and Study Workbook

Prentice
Hall

Needham, Massachusetts
Upper Saddle River, New Jersey
Glenview, Illinois

Prentice Hall

ISBN 0-13-054869-3

6 7 8 9 10   05 04

CONTENTS

① INTRODUCTION TO CHEMISTRY

SECTION 1.1 CHEMISTRY (pages 3–6)

This section defines chemistry and differentiates among its traditional divisions. It also provides several reasons to study chemistry.

▶ What Is Chemistry? (pages 3–4)

1. What is chemistry?

   _____

   _____

   _____

2. What are some applications of chemistry that affect your everyday life?

   _____

   _____

   _____

3. What are the five major subdivisions of chemistry?

   a. _____

   b. _____

   c. _____

   d. _____

   e. _____

4. Is the following sentence true or false? The subdivisions of chemistry often

   overlap. _____

5. Complete the table by filling in the appropriate subdivision of chemistry.

	Investigating a way to make stronger plastic grocery bags
	Developing a better insulin-delivery system for diabetics
	Determining the minerals present in a soil sample
	Using an acid to etch metal
	Creating a cleaner burning heating fuel

CHAPTER 1, Introduction to Chemistry (continued)

▶ **Why Study Chemistry?** (pages 5–6)

6. Why is the study of chemistry important?

_____

_____

7. Circle the letter of each sentence that describes a job that a professional chemist can perform.

    a. A professional chemist can develop new products such as cosmetics.

    b. A professional chemist can help to protect the environment by reducing pollution.

    c. A professional chemist can perform life-saving medical procedures.

    d. A professional chemist can perform quality control in manufacturing.

8. _____ chemistry has specific goals for using scientific

knowledge; _____ chemistry seeks knowledge for its

own sake.

Reading Skill Practice

Outlining can help you understand and remember what you have read. Write an outline for Section 1.1, Chemistry. Begin your outline by copying the headings in the textbook. Under each heading, write the main idea. Then list the details that support the main idea. Do your work on a separate sheet of paper.

SECTION 1.2 CHEMISTRY FAR AND WIDE (pages 7–14)

This section summarizes ways in which chemistry affects your daily life. It also describes the impact of chemistry on various fields.

▶ **Materials** (pages 7–8)

1. One of the most important types of materials in use today is

_____ , which are also called polymers.

2. One of the most important properties of these polymers is their

high _____ ratio.

3. Circle the letter of each fabric that is made from a polymer.

    a. cotton

    b. wool

    c. nylon

    d. polyester

▶ Energy (pages 8–10)

4. List the two ways to meet the ever-growing demand for energy.

    a. _____

    b. _____

5. Because they are a nonrenewable resource, the supply of

    _____ is limited.

6. What inexhaustible source of energy are chemists trying to find new ways to

    capture? _____

7. Circle the letter of the word that identifies what devices chemists have developed to store energy more efficiently.

    a. windmills

    b. new batteries

    c. electric automobiles

    d. new internal-combustion engines

8. Is the following sentence true or false? Nuclear power plants currently use the

    process of nuclear fusion to produce energy. _____

▶ Medicine and Biotechnology (pages 10–11)

9. What is the role of chemistry in the development of medicines?

    _____

    _____

    _____

10. List three new materials chemists have developed that have medical applications.

    a. _____

    b. _____

    c. _____

CHAPTER 1, Introduction to Chemistry *(continued)*

11. Complete the concept map about genes.

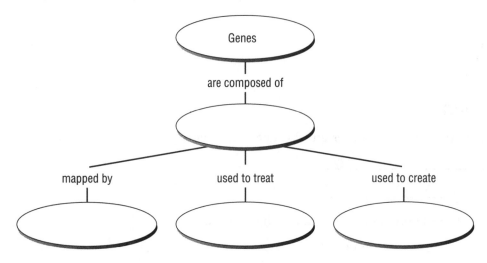

▶ Agriculture *(pages 11–12)*

12. Circle the letter of each sentence that is true about the role of chemistry in agriculture.

    a. Chemists have helped to increase the world's food supply by developing hardier and more productive plants.

    b. Chemists do not study photosynthesis or nitrogen fixation.

    c. Chemists study plant hormones so they can develop better pesticides.

13. How has the discovery of chemicals called pheromones helped to protect plants from insects?

_____

_____

_____

14. Is the following sentence true or false? Insecticides, herbicides, and fungicides used on plants are less specific for the condition they are designed to treat than those developed in the past. _____

▶ The Environment *(pages 12–13)*

15. What are three ways that chemists work to protect the environment?

    a. _____

    b. _____

    c. _____

© Prentice-Hall, Inc.

Match the pollutant with the environmental hazard it creates.

Pollutant	Environmental Hazard
_____ 16. nitrogen oxides	a. acid rain
_____ 17. sulfur compounds	b. ozone depletion
_____ 18. carbon dioxide	c. smog
_____ 19. chlorofluorocarbons	d. global warming

▶ Astronomy and Space Exploration (page 14)

20. Scientists can learn about the chemical composition of stars by analyzing

    their _____ .

21. Why has it been more difficult to discover the chemical composition of the
    moon and planets?

    _____

    _____

    _____

22. What can scientists learn from analyzing the chemical composition of the
    rocks from other planets?

    _____

    _____

    _____

23. Look at Figures 1.16 and 1.17 on page 14. What was the key difference in the
    methods scientists used to analyze rocks from Mars and Earth's moon?

    _____

    _____

SECTION 1.3 THINKING LIKE A SCIENTIST (pages 15–17)

This section describes the steps involved in the scientific method. It also distinguishes between theories and scientific laws.

▶ The Scientific Method (pages 15–16)

1. What is the scientific method?

    _____

    _____

© Prentice-Hall, Inc.

CHAPTER 1, Introduction to Chemistry (continued)

2. Complete the flowchart about the scientific method.

A scientific problem is often discovered when an

_____ is made, which leads to a question.

↓

A _____ is formed when a reason or
explanation is proposed for an observation.

↓

Testing a proposed explanation requires designing an

_____ .

↓

For the results of the test to be accepted, the test must
produce the same results _____ .

↓

An explanation may become a _____ if
the same results are found after many tests.

3. Circle the letter of the activity that involves using the senses to gather information directly.

   a. forming a hypothesis

   b. making an observation

   c. planning an experiment

   d. analyzing data

4. What do scientists do if the results of an experiment do not support the hypothesis?

_____

_____

© Prentice-Hall, Inc.

5. Is the following sentence true or false? Once a theory has been proven, no experiment will ever disprove it. _____

▶ Scientific Laws (page 17)

6. What is a scientific law?

_____

_____

7. Scientific laws can often be expressed by _____ .

8. Circle the letter of each statement that expresses a scientific law.

  a. As the temperature in a cold automobile tire increases, the tire pressure increases.

  b. Increased gas pressure in a sealed container might cause an explosion.

  c. At constant volume, gas pressure is directly proportional to the Kelvin temperature.

  d. The pressure increases when a sealed gas is heated because the energy of the gas particles increases.

SECTION 1.4 HOW TO STUDY CHEMISTRY (pages 20–22)

This section explains why learning chemistry requires daily effort. It also describes the importance of writing in the study of chemistry.

▶ Understanding and Applying Concepts (page 20)

1. What are some skills necessary for learning?

_____

_____

2. Why is it important to learn information that others have discovered?

_____

_____

3. Is the following sentence true or false? An important part of learning is connecting what is learned in the classroom with what happens in the world outside the classroom. _____

▶ Using Your Textbook (page 21)

4. Reading your textbook once helps you get an idea of the overall _____ , but a second, detailed reading, combined with note-taking, is essential for _____ .

CHAPTER 1, Introduction to Chemistry *(continued)*

5. List three ways you can test your knowledge using your textbook.

a. _____

b. _____

c. _____

▶ On Your Own (page 22)

6. What are two strategies you can adopt to enhance your study of chemistry?

a. _____

b. _____

▶ Tests and Quizzes (page 22)

7. Is the following sentence true or false? The best way to study for a test is to cram at the last minute. _____

8. Complete the flowchart on test-taking skills.

Get enough _____ the night before.

↓

Read the test over _____ when you first get it.

↓

Complete the parts of the test that you can answer _____ .

↓

_____ problems that are difficult until the end.

↓

Show _____ when solving numerical problems and _____ your answers to be certain they make sense.

② MATTER AND CHANGE

SECTION 2.1 MATTER (pages 29–31)

This section helps you identify the characteristics of matter and substances. It teaches you how to differentiate among the three states of matter. It also defines a physical property and lists examples of physical properties and physical changes.

▶ Properties of Matter (pages 29–30)

1. What is matter?

_____

2. The _____ of an object is the amount of matter the object contains.

3. Matter that has a uniform and definite composition is called a

_____ .

4. How many kinds of matter does a pure substance contain?

_____

5. Is the following sentence true or false? All samples of a substance have different physical properties. _____

6. A physical property is a quality or condition of a substance that can be

_____ or _____ without

changing the substance's composition.

7. Circle the letter of the term that is NOT a physical property.

   a. odor   **c.** boiling point

   b. density   **d.** melting

8. Look at Table 2.1 on page 29. What is the melting point of bromine? _____

9. Look at Table 2.1 on page 29. Circle the letter of the substance that is a white solid and melts at 185 °C.

   a. sucrose

   b. sodium chloride

   c. sulfur

   d. mercury

10. Is the following sentence true or false? A chemist can help identify a substance

    by its physical properties. _____

CHAPTER 2, Matter and Change *(continued)*

▶ States of Matter (pages 30–31)

11. Circle the letter of the term that is NOT a physical state of matter.

    a. water

    b. gas

    c. liquid

    d. solid

12. Complete the table about properties of the states of matter. Use these terms: *definite, indefinite, moderate, very slight, great, almost,* and *readily.*

Properties of the States of Matter			
Property	**Solid**	**Liquid**	**Gas or Vapor**
Shape		indefinite	
Volume	definite		indefinite
Expansion on heating	very slight		
Compressibility			readily compressible

13. Match each arrangement of the particles in matter with a physical state.

Physical State	**Arrangement**
_____ gas	**a.** packed tightly together
_____ liquid	**b.** close, but not rigidly packed
_____ solid	**c.** spaced far apart

14. Is the following sentence true or false? The words *gas* and *vapor* can be used interchangeably. _____

15. The term gas is limited to those substances that exist in the gaseous state at ordinary _____ .

16. What is vapor?

_____

_____

▶ Physical Changes (page 31)

17. A physical change alters a given material without changing its chemical

_____ .

18. What are some words that describe physical change?

_____

_____

19. What do boiling, freezing, and melting have in common?

_____

SECTION 2.2 MIXTURES (pages 32–35)

This section explains how to categorize a sample of matter as a substance or a mixture. It also teaches you how to distinguish between homogeneous and heterogeneous samples of matter.

▶ Classifying Mixtures (pages 32–33)

1. Is the following sentence true or false? Most samples of matter are mixtures.

_____

2. What is a mixture?

_____

3. Is the following sentence true or false? A heterogeneous mixture is one that

has a completely uniform composition. _____

4. What is another name for a homogeneous mixture?

_____

5. Which physical state, if any, cannot exist in a solution?

_____

6. Circle the letter of the term that describes a part of a system with uniform composition and properties.

    a. solution

    b. mixture

    c. state

    d. phase

CHAPTER 2, Matter and Change (continued)

7. How many phases exist in these types of mixtures?

   a. Homogeneous _____

   b. Heterogeneous _____

Match each type of solution with an example of it.

_____ **8.** solid-solid   **a.** sugar water

_____ **9.** solid-liquid   **b.** vinegar

_____ **10.** liquid-liquid   **c.** carbon mixed with iron to form steel

_____ **11.** gas-liquid   **d.** soda water

_____ **12.** gas-gas   **e.** air

▶ Separating Mixtures (pages 33–34)

13. Is the following sentence true or false? It is always easy to separate the
    components in mixtures. _____

14. What is distillation?

    _____

Match each term with its location in the diagram.

_____ **15.** condenser

_____ **16.** heat source

_____ **17.** thermometer

_____ **18.** impure solution

_____ **19.** distilled liquid

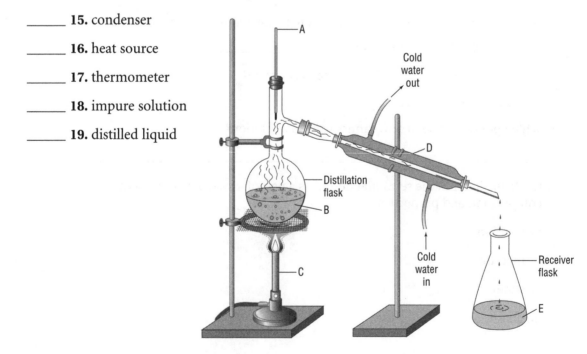

Reading Skill Practice

By looking carefully at photographs and drawings in textbooks, you can better understand what you have read. Look carefully at Figure 2.5 on page 34. What important idea does this drawing communicate?

SECTION 2.3 ELEMENTS AND COMPOUNDS (pages 36–40)

This section explains the difference between an element and a compound. It also helps you identify the chemical symbols of common elements, and name common elements, given their symbols.

▶ **Distinguishing Elements and Compounds** (pages 36–39)

1. What are the two groups into which substances can be classified?

   _____

   _____

   _____

2. Is the following sentence true or false? Elements can be separated easily into simpler substances. _____

3. Compounds are substances that can be separated into simpler substances only by _____ means.

4. Is the following sentence true or false? The properties of compounds are different from those of their component elements. _____

5. Use Figure 2.7 on page 37 and its caption to help you complete this sentence. Table salt (sodium chloride) is a _____ of sodium, a soft _____ , and chlorine, a _____ .

6. Describe one way to decide whether a sample of matter is a substance or a mixture.

   _____

   _____

   _____

© Prentice-Hall, Inc.

CHAPTER 2, Matter and Change *(continued)*

7. Complete the labels in the diagram below.

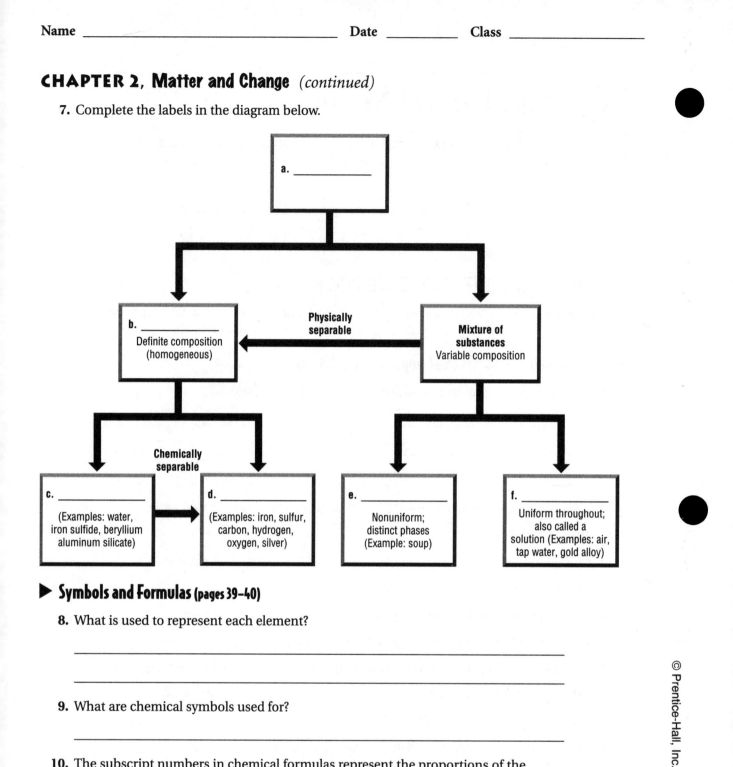

▶ Symbols and Formulas *(pages 39–40)*

8. What is used to represent each element?

_____

_____

9. What are chemical symbols used for?

_____

10. The subscript numbers in chemical formulas represent the proportions of the various elements in the _____ .

11. Is the following sentence true or false? The elements that make up a compound are always present in the same proportions. _____

© Prentice-Hall, Inc.

12. Use Table 2.4 on page 40 to answer the following questions.

    a. Pb is the symbol for what element? _____

    b. What is the symbol for gold? _____

    c. Stibium is the Latin name for which element? _____

SECTION 2.4 CHEMICAL REACTIONS (pages 41–43)

This section helps you differentiate between physical and chemical changes in matter. It also teaches you how to apply the law of conservation of mass.

▶ Changing Reactants to Products (pages 41–42)

1. What happens in a chemical reaction?

_____

2. In chemical reactions, the starting substances are called

_____ and the substances formed are

called _____ .

3. What is a chemical property?

_____

_____

_____

4. Is the following sentence true or false? Chemical properties are observed only

when a substance undergoes a chemical change. _____

5. Circle the letter of the term that best completes the sentence. A chemical
change _____ results in a change in chemical composition of the substances
involved.

    a. sometimes

    b. rarely

    c. always

    d. never

6. What are some words that describe chemical change?

_____

_____

CHAPTER 2, Matter and Change *(continued)*

7. Which representation of a chemical reaction is correct?

    a. products ➞ reactants

    b. reactants ➞ products

8. Complete the flowchart below, which describes the process of determining whether a chemical reaction has taken place.

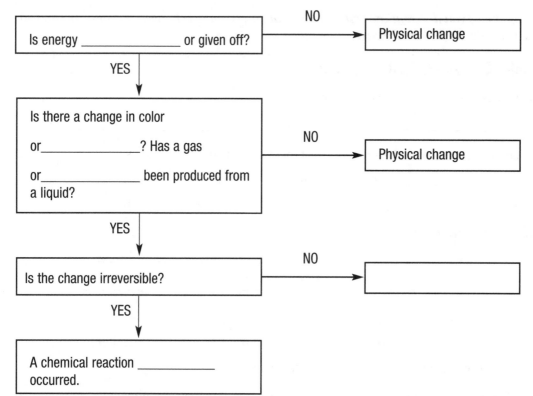

NO

Is energy _____ or given off?   →   Physical change

YES

Is there a change in color

or_____? Has a gas   NO

or_____ been produced from   →   Physical change
a liquid?

YES

Is the change irreversible?   NO   →

YES

A chemical reaction _____
occurred.

▶ Conservation of Mass *(page 43)*

9. During a chemical reaction, the mass of products is always equal to the mass

of _____ .

10. How was the law of conservation of mass determined?

_____

11. The law of conservation of mass states that in any physical change or

chemical reaction, mass is neither _____ nor

_____ .

12. Look at Figure 2.12 on page 43. Explain how it is easier to demonstrate the law of conservation of mass with a flashbulb than with a burning match.

_____

© Prentice-Hall, Inc.

3 SCIENTIFIC MEASUREMENT

SECTION 3.1 THE IMPORTANCE OF MEASUREMENT (pages 51–53)

This section explains the difference between qualitative and quantitative measurements, and how scientific notation can help express very large or very small numbers.

▶ Qualitative and Quantitative Measurements (page 51)

1. The system of units used for measurements in chemistry is called the

   _____ .

2. Is the following statement true or false? A qualitative measurement gives a

   precise, numerical result. _____

3. Is the following statement true or false? A quantitative measurement gives a

   result in a definite form, usually as a number and a unit. _____

Five types of measurements you might make are described below. Label each sentence that describes a qualitative measurement as QUAL. Label each sentence that describes a quantitative measurement as QUAN.

_____ 4. You touch another person's forehead and say, "You feel feverish."

_____ 5. You need cut to wood to make a shelf for a bookcase. You use a tape measure to mark off a 50-centimeter length of wood.

_____ 6. With a thermometer, you find that you have a temperature of 39.0 °C.

_____ 7. After visually observing a car speed down a street, you exclaim to a friend that the car was traveling "way too fast."

_____ 8. You hold two rocks, one in each hand, and say, "The rock in my right hand is heavier."

9. State one reason quantitative measurements can be more useful than qualitative measurements.

   _____

   _____

   _____

   _____

   _____

CHAPTER 3, Scientific Measurement *(continued)*

▶ Scientific Notation (pages 52–53)

10. Look at Figure 3.3 on page 52. Why are numbers used in chemistry usually expressed in scientific notation?

_____

_____

_____

_____

11. Circle the letter of each sentence that is true about numbers expressed in scientific notation.

   a. A number expressed in scientific notation is written as the product of a coefficient and a power of 10.

   b. The power of 10 is called the exponent.

   c. The coefficient is always a number greater than or equal to one and less than ten.

   d. For numbers less than one, the exponent is positive.

12. Circle the letter of the answer in which 503 000 000 is written correctly in scientific notation.

   a. 5.03×10^{-7}

   b. 503×10^{6}

   c. 5.03×10^{8}

   d. 503 million

13. Draw an arrow beneath 0.000 76 in the equation below to show the place to which the decimal point moves. Then answer the questions.

$$0.00076 = 7.6 \times 10^{\boxed{?}}$$

   a. How many places did the decimal point move? in which direction?

   _____

   b. To make the equation true, does 7.6 need to be multiplied by a number greater than one or less than one? _____

   c. Is the exponent for 10 positive or negative? _____

   d. What exponent makes the equation true? _____

14. Draw an arrow beneath 76 000 000 in the equation below to show the place to which the decimal point moves. Then answer the questions.

$$76\ 000\ 000 = 7.6 \times 10^{\boxed{?}}$$

a. What direction did the decimal point move? _____

b. To make a true equation, does 7.6 need to be multiplied by a number greater than one or less than one? _____

c. Is the exponent for 10 positive or negative? _____

d. What exponent makes the equation true? _____

SECTION 3.2 UNCERTAINTY IN MEASUREMENTS (pages 54–62)

This section describes the concepts of accuracy, precision, and error in measurements. It also explains the proper use of significant figures in measurements and calculations.

▶ Accuracy, Precision, and Error (pages 54–55)

1. Is the following sentence true or false? To decide whether a measurement has good precision or poor precision, the measurement must be made more than once. _____

Label each of the three following sentences that describes accuracy with an *A*. Label each sentence that describes precision with a *P.*

_____ **2.** Four of five repetitions of a measurement were numerically identical, and the fifth varied from the others in value by less than 1%.

_____ **3.** Eight measurements were spread over a wide range.

_____ **4.** A single measurement is within 1% of the correct value.

5. On a dartboard, darts that are closest to the bull's-eye have been thrown with the greatest accuracy. On the second target, draw three darts to represent three tosses of lower precision, but higher accuracy than the darts on the first target.

First target

Second target

CHAPTER 3, Scientific Measurement *(continued)*

6. What is the meaning of "accepted value" with respect to an experimental measurement?

_____

7. Complete the following sentence. For an experimental measurement, the accepted value minus the experimental value is called the _____ .

8. Is the following sentence true or false? The value of an error must be positive. _____

9. Relative error is also called _____ .

10. The accepted value of a length measurement is 200 cm, and the experimental value is 198 cm. Circle the letter of the value that shows the percent error of this measurement.

　　a. 2%

　　b. −2%

　　c. 1%

　　d. −1%

▶ Significant Figures in Measurements (pages 56–58)

11. If a thermometer is calibrated to the nearest degree, to what part of a degree can you estimate the temperature it measures? _____

12. Circle the letter of the correct digit. In the measurement 43.52 cm, which digit is the most uncertain?

　　a. 4 　　　　**c.** 5

　　b. 3 　　　　**d.** 2

13. Circle the letter of the correct number of significant figures in the measurement 6.80 m.

　　a. 2 　　　　**c.** 4

　　b. 3 　　　　**d.** 5

14. List two situations in which measurements have an unlimited number of significant figures.

　　a. _____

　　b. _____

　　　　_____

　　　　_____

15. Circle the letter of each sentence that is true about significant figures.

    a. Every nonzero digit in a reported measurement is assumed to be significant.

    b. Zeros appearing between nonzero digits are never significant.

    c. Leftmost zeros acting as placeholders in front of nonzero digits in numbers less than one are not significant.

    d. All rightmost zeros to the right of the decimal point are always significant.

    e. Zeros to the left of the decimal point that act as placeholders for the first nonzero digit to the left of the decimal point are not significant.

▶ Significant Figures in Calculations (pages 58–61)

16. Is the following sentence true or false? An answer is as precise as the most precise measurement from which it was calculated. _____

Round the following measurements as indicated.

17. Round 65.145 meters to 4 significant figures. _____

18. Round 100.1 °C to 1 significant figure. _____

19. Round 155 cm to two significant figures. _____

20. Round 0.000 718 kilograms to two significant figures. _____

21. Round 65.145 meters to three significant figures. _____

SECTION 3.3 INTERNATIONAL SYSTEM OF UNITS (pages 63–67)

This section defines units of measurement for length, volume, and mass in the International System of Units (SI).

▶ Units of Length (pages 63–64)

1. Complete the table showing selected SI base units of measurement.

Units of Measurement		
Quantity	SI base unit	Symbol
Length		
Mass		
Temperature		
Time		

CHAPTER 3, Scientific Measurement (continued)

2. All metric units of length are based on multiples of _____ .

3. The International System of Units (SI) is a revised version of the

_____ .

4. Explain what is meant by a "derived unit."

_____

_____

_____

5. Give at least one example of a derived unit.

_____

_____

_____

6. Complete the following table showing some metric units of length. Remember that the meter is the SI base unit for length.

Metric Units of Length		
Unit	**Symbol**	**Factor Multiplying Base Unit**
Meter	m	1
Kilometer		
Centimeter		
Millimeter		
Nanometer		

Match each metric unit with the best estimate of its length or distance.

_____ **7.** Height of a stove top above the floor   **a.** 1 km

_____ **8.** Thickness of about 10 sheets of paper   **b.** 1 m

_____ **9.** Distance along a road spanning about 10 telephone poles   **c.** 1 cm

_____ **10.** Width of a key on a computer keyboard   **d.** 1 mm

▶ Units of Volume (pages 65–66)

11. The space occupied by any sample of matter is called its _____ .

12. Circle the letter of each sentence that is true about units of volume.

    a. The SI unit for volume is derived from the meter, the SI unit for length.

    b. The liter (L) is a unit of volume.

    c. The liter is an SI unit.

    d. There are 1000 cm^3 in 1 L, and there are also 1000 mL in 1 L, so 1 cm^3 is equal to 1 mL.

Match each of the three descriptions of a volume to the appropriate metric unit of volume.

	Example	Unit of Volume
_____	**13.** Interior of an oven	**a.** 1 L
_____	**14.** A box of cookies	**b.** 1 m^3
_____	**15.** One-quarter teaspoon	**c.** 1 mL

16. Circle the letter of each type of volumetric glassware that can be used to make accurate measurements of liquid volume.

    a. graduated cylinder

    b. pipet

    c. buret

17. The volume of any solid, liquid, or gas will change with

_____ .

▶ Units of Mass (pages 66–67)

18. Is the following sentence true or false? The mass of an object changes with

location. _____

19. When brought to the surface of the moon, will a mass have more or less weight than it did on the surface of Earth, or will it be the same weight? Explain.

_____

_____

20. A kilogram was originally defined as the mass of _____ .

21. Circle the letter of the unit of mass commonly used in chemistry that equals 1/1000 kilogram.

    a. gram   **b.** milligram   **c.** milliliter

CHAPTER 3, Scientific Measurement *(continued)*

Match each unit of mass with the object whose mass would be closest to that unit.

	Mass	Unit of Mass
_____	**22.** A few grains of sand	**a.** 1 kg
_____	**23.** A liter bottle of soda	**b.** 1 g
_____	**24.** Five aspirin tablets	**c.** 1 mg

25. Look at Figure 3.14 on page 67. Circle the letter of the instrument shown that is used to measure mass.

   a. scale

   b. balance beam

   c. platform balance

   d. analytical balance

SECTION 3.4 DENSITY (pages 68–72)

This section defines density and specific gravity. It explains that density is a characteristic property that depends on the composition of a substance, not on the size of the sample.

▶ Determining Density (page 68–71)

1. Is the mass of one pound of lead greater than, less than, or equal to the mass

   of one pound of feathers? _____

2. Which material has a greater density, lead or feathers? _____

3. How is density defined?

   _____

4. The mass of a sample is measured in grams, and its volume is measured in cubic centimeters. In what units would its density be reported?

   _____

5. Look at Table 3.7 on page 69. Circle the letter of the material that will sink in liquid water at 4 °C.

   a. aluminum

   b. corn oil

   c. ice

   d. gasoline

6. The density of a substance generally decreases as its temperature increases. Are there any exceptions to this statement? Explain.

_____

_____

_____

▶ Specific Gravity (page 72)

7. What is specific gravity?

_____

_____

8. Do all substances have a specific gravity? Explain.

_____

_____

9. What is the material commonly used as a reference for calculation of specific

gravity? _____

10. Why does specific gravity have no units?

_____

_____

Use the instrument shown below to answer Questions 11 and 12.

11. The instrument is used to measure specific gravity.

What is it called? _____

12. Draw an arrow to show the point at which you read the scale.

SECTION 3.5 TEMPERATURE (pages 74–75)

This section describes the concept of temperature and explains how temperature is measured.

▶ Measuring Temperature (page 74)

1. Draw an arrow below the diagram, showing the direction of heat transfer between two objects.

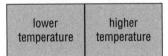

2. What properties explain the behavior of liquid-filled thermometers?

_____

_____

_____

_____

▶ Temperature Scales (page 74)

3. What are the two reference temperatures on the Celsius scale?

_____

_____

4. What is the zero point, 0 K, on the Kelvin scale called?

_____

5. A change of temperature equal to one Kelvin is equal to a change of

temperature of how many degrees Celsius? _____

6. Complete the diagram to show the reference temperatures in the Celsius and Kelvin scales.

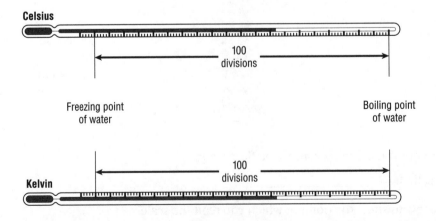

GUIDED PRACTICE PROBLEM 7 (page 59)

7. Round 87.073 meters to three significant figures. Write your answer in scientific notation.

   Step 1. To round to three significant figures, round to the nearest tenth.

   87.073 rounds to _____

   Step 2. Write the number in scientific notation.

   _____ meters

GUIDED PRACTICE PROBLEM 23 (page 71)

23. A student finds a shiny piece of metal that she thinks is aluminum. In the lab, she determines that the metal has a volume of 245 cm^3 and a mass of 612 g. Calculate the density. Is the metal aluminum?

Analyze

   Step 1. List the known values.

   Volume = 245 cm^3

   Mass = _____ g

   Step 2. List the unknown.

   _____

Calculate

   Step 3. Use the following relationship to find the density. Remember to round your answer to three significant figures.

   $$\text{Density} = \frac{\text{mass}}{\text{volume}}$$

   $$= \frac{612 \text{ g}}{\_\_\_\_ \text{ cm}^3}$$

   $$= \_\_\_\_ \text{ g/cm}^3$$

   Step 4. To determine whether the piece of metal is aluminum, compare the density of the metal to the density of aluminum given in Table 3.6 on

   page 68. Is the metal aluminum? _____

Evaluate

   Step 5. Underline the correct word(s) that complete(s) this statement. Because the mass of the metal is about two and one-half times the volume, a density of about 2.5 g/cm^3 is reasonable. Because a density of 2.50 g/cm^3 is nearly 10% less than 2.7 g/cm^3, the density of aluminum, the metal (is, is not) aluminum.

4 PROBLEM SOLVING IN CHEMISTRY

SECTION 4.1 WHAT DO I DO NOW? (pages 83–88)

This section explains useful problem-solving skills. It also describes a suggested three-step problem-solving approach.

▶ Skills Used in Solving Problems (page 83)

1. What is one way to become a better problem solver?

_____

2. Name an everyday situation that requires problem-solving skills.

_____

_____

3. Why is it important to develop a plan for problem solving?

_____

_____

▶ A Three-Step Problem-Solving Approach (pages 84–88)

4. What are the three steps suggested for solving problems?

    a. _____

    b. _____

    c. _____

5. For the following word problem, fill in the table, listing the known and unknown information: Ethylene glycol, an ingredient in antifreeze, has a density of 1.1135 g/cm^3 at 20 °C. If you need 500 mL of this liquid, what mass, in grams, is required?

Known	Unknown

© Prentice-Hall, Inc.

CHAPTER 4, Problem Solving in Chemistry *(continued)*

6. Riddles are often written to give the problem solver so much information that what is known becomes confused with what is unknown. How can you avoid this confusion?

_____

_____

_____

7. What are some steps that may need to be performed to calculate an answer to a problem?

_____

_____

_____

8. List three questions that can be asked when evaluating an answer.

_____

_____

_____

9. An unknown piece of metal, with a mass of 65.315 g, is 2.87 cm long, 1.54 cm wide, and 1.09 cm thick. Describe how you could calculate the volume and the density of the metal.

_____

_____

_____

SECTION 4.2 SIMPLE CONVERSION PROBLEMS (pages 89–95)

This section explains how to construct conversion factors from equivalent measurements. It also describes how to apply the techniques of dimensional analysis to a variety of conversion problems.

▶ Conversion Factors (pages 89–90)

1. How are the two parts of a conversion factor related?

_____

2. Look at Figure 4.4. In a conversion factor, the smaller number is part of the quantity that has the _____ unit. The larger number is part of the quantity that has the _____ unit.

© Prentice-Hall, Inc.

3. Is the following sentence true or false? The actual size of a measurement multiplied by a conversion factor remains the same, because the measurement being converted is multiplied by unity. _____

4. Write two conversion factors based on the relationship between hours and minutes.

_____

5. The average lead for a mechanical pencil is 6.0 cm long when it is new. Circle the letter of the conversion factor you would use to find its length in inches.

a. $\dfrac{2.54 \text{ cm}}{1 \text{ in.}}$

b. $\dfrac{1 \text{ in.}}{2.54 \text{ cm}}$

c. $\dfrac{1 \text{ in.}}{6.0 \text{ cm}}$

d. $\dfrac{6.0 \text{ cm}}{1 \text{ in.}}$

6. A student is asked to calculate the volume, in milliliters, of 2 cups of oil. There are 225 mL per cup. The student calculates the volume as follows:

$$\text{Volume} = 2 \text{ cups} \times \frac{1 \text{ cup}}{25 \text{ mL}} = 0.08 \text{ cup}$$

List three errors the student made.

_____

_____

_____

▶ Dimensional Analysis (pages 90–93)

7. What is dimensional analysis?

_____

_____

_____

8. Reread Sample Problem 4.3. The correct conversion factor has the _____ unit in the denominator and the _____ unit in the numerator.

9. Look at Figure 4.6 and its caption. Set up the calculation you would use to solve this problem.

_____

CHAPTER 4, Problem Solving in Chemistry *(continued)*

10. What are the units for the answer to Question 9? _____

11. Complete the table to show the units you need to use for volume or density based on the known units. Use dimensional analysis.

Mass	Volume	Density
g	cm^3	
kg	m^3	
kg		$\dfrac{kg}{km^3}$

12. A container can hold 65 g of water. Circle the conversion factor needed to find the mass of water that 5 identical containers can hold.

a. $\dfrac{5 \text{ containers}}{65 \text{ g water}}$

b. $\dfrac{1 \text{ container}}{65 \text{ g water}}$

c. $\dfrac{65 \text{ g water}}{1 \text{ container}}$

d. $\dfrac{65 \text{ g water}}{5 \text{ containers}}$

▶ Converting Between Units (pages 93–95)

13. Converting between units is easily done using _____ .

14. Circle the letter of the conversion factor that you would use to convert tablespoons to milliliters.

a. $\dfrac{4 \text{ fluid ounces}}{1 \text{ tablespoon}}$

b. $\dfrac{1 \text{ tablespoon}}{4 \text{ fluid ounces}}$

c. $\dfrac{1 \text{ tablespoon}}{15 \text{ mL}}$

d. $\dfrac{15 \text{ mL}}{1 \text{ tablespoon}}$

15. Show the calculation you would use to convert the following:

a. 0.25 m to centimeters

_____

b. 9.8 g to kilograms

_____

c. 35 ms to seconds

_____

d. 4.2 dL to liters

_____

SECTION 4.3 MORE COMPLEX PROBLEMS (pages 97–100)

This section describes how to solve problems by breaking the solution into steps. It also explains how to use dimensional analysis to convert complex units.

▶ Multistep Problems (pages 97–98)

1. Complex conversions between units may require using _____ conversion factor.

2. How many conversion factors would you need to use to find the number of liters in a cubic decimeter? What are they?

_____

_____

3. How would you calculate the number of nanometers in 8.1 cm?

_____

4. What is the equivalent of 0.35 lb in grams?

_____

5. A scientist has 0.46 mL of a solution. How would she convert this volume to microliters?

_____

6. Describe the steps you would use to solve this problem. In a scale drawing of a dining room floor plan, 10 mm equals 2 meters. If the homeowners wanted to purchase flooring that costs $10.89 per square yard, how much would they spend on flooring for the dining room? The dimensions of the dining room on the floor plan are 40 mm × 32 mm.

_____

_____

_____

© Prentice-Hall, Inc.

CHAPTER 4, Problem Solving in Chemistry *(continued)*

▶ Converting Complex Units *(page 99)*

7. Name three common measurements that are expressed as a ratio of two units.

_____

8. What technique can be used to convert complex units?

_____

9. A normal concentration of glucose, or sugar, in the blood is 95 mg/dL. How many grams of sugar would be present per liter of blood? Show the conversion factors you use.

_____

10. Replace each question mark in the table with the conversion factors needed to obtain the given units of density.

Mass	Volume	Density
g	$mm^3 \times \ ?$	g/m^3
$kg \times \ ?$	$cm^3 \times \ ?$	g/m^3

11. A man can run a mile in 4 minutes. Calculate his average speed in kilometers per hour. Show your work. (1 mile = 1.61 km)

_____

_____

12. A baseball player's batting average is .254 (254 hits per 1000 at bats). If she is at bat an average of 3 times per game, how many hits will she make in 52 games? Show your work.

_____

_____

Reading Skill Practice

By looking carefully at photographs and illustrations in your textbook, you can better understand what you have read. Look carefully at Figure 4.8 on page 98. What important idea does this illustration communicate? Do your work on a separate sheet of paper.

© Prentice-Hall, Inc.

GUIDED PRACTICE PROBLEM 1 (page 88)

1. The density of silicon is 2.33 g/cm³. What is the volume of a piece of silicon that has a mass of 62.9 g?

Analyze

Step 1. What is the equation for density? _____

Step 2. Which values are given in the problem? _____

Step 3. What value do you need to find? _____

Calculate

Step 4. Multiply both sides of the equation for density by $\dfrac{\text{volume}}{\text{density}}$ to solve for volume.

Step 5. Substitute the given measurements into the new equation. Calculate the volume. Round your answer to three significant figures.

Answer: _____

Evaluate

Step 6. Explain why you think your answer is reasonable.

_____

_____

Step 7. Are the units in your answer correct? How do you know?

_____

_____

CHAPTER 4, Problem Solving in Chemistry *(continued)*

EXTRA PRACTICE (similar to Practice Problem 13a, page 94)

13a. Use dimensional analysis to convert 4.68 g of boron to cubic centimeters of boron. The density of boron is 2.34 g/cm^3.

GUIDED PRACTICE PROBLEM 20 (page 97)

20. The radius of a potassium atom is 0.227 nm.
Express this radius in centimeters.
Complete the following steps to solve the problem.

Step 1. Use the conversion factors for nanometers and centimeters.

$$0.227 \text{ nm} \times \frac{\boxed{}}{1 \times 10^9 \text{ nm}} \times \boxed{}$$

Step 2. Simplify.

$$= \frac{0.227 \times 10^2}{10^9} \boxed{}$$

Step 3. Divide.

$$= \boxed{} \text{ cm}$$

EXTRA PRACTICE (similar to Practice Problem 23, page 98)

23. How many centimeters are in 2 km?

EXTRA PRACTICE (similar to Practice Problem 24, page 99)

24. Gold has a density of about 20 g/cm^3. Estimate this density in kg/m^3.

© Prentice-Hall, Inc.

5 ATOMIC STRUCTURE AND THE PERIODIC TABLE

SECTION 5.1 ATOMS (pages 107–108)

This section describes early atomic theories of matter and provides ways to understand the tiny size of individual atoms.

▶ Early Models of the Atom (pages 107–108)

1. Democritus of Abdera, who lived in Greece during the fourth century B.C., suggested that matter is made up of tiny particles that cannot be divided. He called these particles _____ .

2. List two reasons why the ideas of Democritus were not useful in a scientific

   sense. _____

   _____

3. The modern process of discovery about atoms began with the theories of an

   English schoolteacher named _____ .

4. Circle the letter of each sentence that is true about Dalton's atomic theory.

   a. All elements are composed of tiny, indivisible particles called atoms.

   b. An element is composed of several types of atoms.

   c. Atoms of different elements can physically mix together, or can chemically combine in simple, whole-number ratios to form compounds.

   d. Chemical reactions occur when atoms are separated, joined, or rearranged; however, atoms of one element are never changed into atoms of another element by a chemical reaction.

5. In the diagram, use the labels *mixture* and *compound* to identify the mixture of elements A and B and the compound that forms when the atoms of elements A and B combine chemically.

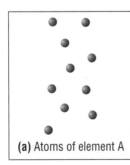
(a) Atoms of element A

(b) Atoms of element B

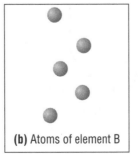
_____

_____

CHAPTER 5, Atomic Structure and the Periodic Table *(continued)*

▶ Just How Small Is an Atom? (page 108)

6. Suppose you could grind a sample of the element copper into smaller and smaller particles. The smallest particle that could no longer be divided, yet still has the properties of copper, is _____ .

7. About how many atoms of copper when placed side by side would form a line 1 cm long? _____

SECTION 5.2 STRUCTURE OF THE NUCLEAR ATOM (pages 109–112)

This section describes the experiments that led to the discovery of subatomic particles and their properties.

▶ Electrons (pages 109–110)

1. How is the atomic theory that is accepted today different from Dalton's atomic theory? _____

_____

2. Which subatomic particles carry a negative charge? _____

Match each term from the experiments of J. J. Thomson with the correct description.

_____ **3.** anode   **a.** an electrode with a negative charge

_____ **4.** cathode   **b.** a glowing beam traveling between charged electrodes

_____ **5.** cathode ray   **c.** an electrode with a positive charge

_____ **6.** electron   **d.** a negatively charged particle

7. The diagram shows electrons moving from left to right in a cathode-ray tube. Draw an arrow showing how the path of the electrons will be affected by the placement of the negatively and positively charged plates.

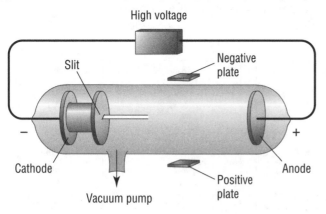

© Prentice-Hall, Inc.

8. Thomson observed that the production of cathode rays did not depend on the kind of gas in the tube or the type of metal used for the electrodes. What conclusion did he draw from these observations?

_____

9. What two properties of an electron did Robert Millikan determine from his experiments?

_____

▶ Protons and Neutrons (pages 110–111)

10. Circle the letter of each sentence that is true about atoms, matter, and electric charge.

    a. All atoms have an electric charge.

    b. Electric charges are carried by particles of matter.

    c. Electric charges always exist in whole-number multiples of a single basic unit.

    d. When a given number of positively charged particles combines with an equal number of negatively charged particles, an electrically neutral particle is formed.

11. Circle the letter next to the number of units of positive charge that remain if a hydrogen atom loses an electron.

    a. 0   b. 1   c. 2   d. 3

12. The positively charged subatomic particle that remains when a hydrogen atom loses an electron is called _____ .

13. What charge does a neutron carry? _____ .

14. Complete the table about the properties of subatomic particles.

Properties of Subatomic Particles				
Particle	Symbol	Relative Electrical Charge	Relative Mass (mass of proton = 1)	Actual Mass (g)
Electron	e^-			9.11×10^{-28}
Proton	p^+			1.67×10^{-24}
Neutron	n^0			1.67×10^{-24}

CHAPTER 5, Atomic Structure and the Periodic Table *(continued)*

▶ The Atomic Nucleus (pages 111–112)

15. Is the following sentence true or false? An alpha particle has a double positive

charge because it is a helium atom that has lost two electrons. _____

16. Explain why in 1911 Rutherford and his coworkers were surprised when they shot a narrow beam of alpha particles through a thin sheet of gold foil.

_____

_____

_____

_____

_____

17. Circle the letter of each sentence that is true about the nuclear theory of atoms suggested by Rutherford's experimental results.

a. An atom is mostly empty space.

b. All the positive charge of an atom is concentrated in a small central region called the nucleus.

c. The nucleus is composed of protons.

d. The nucleus is large compared with the atom as a whole.

e. Nearly all the mass of an atom is in its nucleus.

SECTION 5.3 DISTINGUISHING BETWEEN ATOMS (pages 113–121)

This section explains how atomic number identifies an element; how to use atomic number and mass number to find the number of protons, neutrons, and electrons in an atom; how isotopes differ; and how to calculate average atomic mass.

▶ Atomic Number (page 113)

1. Circle the letter of the term that correctly completes the sentence. Elements are different because their atoms contain different numbers of _____ .

a. electrons

b. protons

c. neutrons

d. nuclei

© Prentice-Hall, Inc.

2. Complete the table showing the number of protons and electrons in atoms of six elements.

Atoms of Six Elements				
Name	**Symbol**	**Atomic Number**	**Number of Protons**	**Number of Electrons**
Hydrogen	H	1		
Helium	He		2	
Lithium	Li	3		
Boron	B	5		
Carbon	C	6		
Oxygen	O			8

▶ Mass Number (pages 115–116)

3. The total number of protons and neutrons in an atom is its

   _____ .

4. What is the mass number of a helium atom that has two protons and two

   neutrons? _____

5. How many neutrons does a beryllium atom with four protons and a mass

   number of nine have? _____

6. Place the labels *chemical symbol, atomic number,* and *mass number* in the
   shorthand notation below.

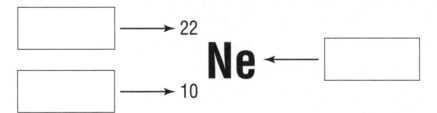

7. Designate the atom shown in Question 6 in the form "name of element"-"mass

   number." _____

8. How many protons, neutrons, and electrons are in the atom discussed in

   Questions 6 and 7? Protons: [   ] Neutrons: [   ] Electrons: [   ]

CHAPTER 5, Atomic Structure and the Periodic Table *(continued)*

▶ Isotopes (pages 116–117)

9. How do atoms of neon-20 and neon-22 differ?

   _____

   _____

10. Neon-20 and neon-22 are called _____ .

11. Is the following sentence true or false? Isotopes are chemically alike because

    they have identical numbers of protons and electrons. _____

Match the designation of each hydrogen isotope with its commonly used name.

   _____ **12.** hydrogen-1   **a.** tritium

   _____ **13.** hydrogen-2   **b.** hydrogen

   _____ **14.** hydrogen-3   **c.** deuterium

▶ Atomic Mass (pages 118–121)

15. Why is the atomic mass unit (amu), rather than the gram, usually used to express atomic mass?

    _____

    _____

16. What isotope of carbon has been chosen as the reference isotope for atomic mass units? What is the defined atomic mass in amu of this isotope?

    _____

17. Is the following sentence true or false? The atomic mass of an element is

    always a whole number of atomic mass units. _____

18. Circle the letter of each statement that is true about the average atomic mass of an element and the relative abundance of its isotopes.

    a. In nature, most elements occur as a mixture of two or more isotopes.

    b. Isotopes of an element do not have a specific natural percent abundance.

    c. The average atomic mass of an element is usually closest to that of the isotope with the highest natural abundance.

    d. Because hydrogen has three isotopes with atomic masses of about 1 amu, 2 amu, and 3 amu, respectively, the average atomic mass of natural hydrogen is 2 amu.

19. Circle the letter of the correct answer. When chlorine occurs in nature, there are three atoms of chlorine-35 for every one atom of chlorine-37. Which atomic mass number is closer to the average atomic mass of chlorine?

    a. 35 amu   **b.** 37 amu

© Prentice-Hall, Inc.

Reading Skill Practice

Outlining can help you understand and remember what you have read. Prepare an outline of Section 5.3, *Distinguishing Between Atoms.* Begin with the headings in the textbook. Under each heading, write the main idea. Then list the details that support the main idea. Do your work on a separate sheet of paper.

SECTION 5.4   THE PERIODIC TABLE: ORGANIZING THE ELEMENTS
(pages 123–126)

This section describes the development of the periodic table and explains the arrangement of groups and periods in the modern periodic table.

▶ Development of the Periodic Table (page 123)

1. About how many elements had been discovered by the mid-1800s? _____

2. Who was Dmitri Mendeleev? _____

_____

_____

3. What variable did Mendeleev use to organize his version of the periodic table?

_____

4. Is the following sentence true or false? Mendeleev and other scientists were

able to use the periodic table to predict the properties of undiscovered

elements. _____

5. How did Moseley change the periodic table?

_____

▶ The Modern Periodic Table (pages 124–126)

6. Explain the color coding of the symbols in the periodic table on page 124.

_____

_____

_____

_____

CHAPTER 5, Atomic Structure and the Periodic Table *(continued)*

7. Label the sample square from the periodic table below. Use the labels *name of element, chemical symbol, atomic number,* and *atomic mass.*

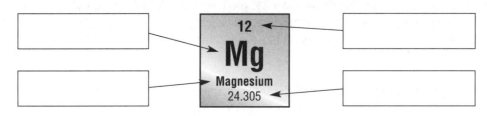

8. Use the data in Question 7 to determine how many protons are in the nucleus of each atom of magnesium. _____

9. The horizontal rows in the periodic table are called _____ .

10. Is the following statement true or false? The periodic law states that when elements are arranged in order of increasing atomic number, there is a periodic repetition of physical and chemical properties. _____

11. Why are Group A elements called representative elements?

_____

12. Complete the table concerning general properties of the broad classes of elements.

Class of Elements	General Properties
Metals	
Nonmetals	
Metalloids	properties are intermediate between metals and nonmetals

13. Classify each of the following elements as a (an) *alkali metal, alkaline earth metal, transition metal, halogen, noble gas,* or *metalloid.* Draw lines connecting elements in this table that have similar properties.

a. sodium _____

b. germanium _____

c. calcium _____

d. fluorine _____

e. xenon _____

f. copper _____

g. chlorine _____

h. silicon _____

j. potassium _____

k. magnesium _____

MathWise

Fill in the write-on lines and boxes provided as you work through the guided practice problems.

GUIDED PRACTICE PROBLEM 10 (page 116)

10. Use Table 5.2 and Figure 5.8 to express the compositions of carbon-12 and fluorine-19 in shorthand notation.

Analyze

Carbon-12

Step 1. The number of protons in an atom is called its _____ number.

The number of protons in an atom of carbon-12 is _____ .

Step 2. The number of protons plus the number of neutrons in an atom is called

its _____ number. For carbon-12, this number is _____ .

Solve

Step 3. The shorthand notation for carbon-12 is:

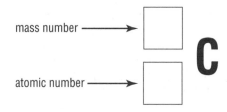

Evaluate

Step 4. Except for hydrogen-1, the mass number of an isotope is always greater

than its atomic number. Is the mass number reasonable? _____

Fluorine-19

Step 1. The atomic number of fluorine-19 is _____ .

Step 2. Its mass number is _____ .

Step 3. The shorthand notation for fluorine-19 is: [ ] [ ] **F**

Step 4. Is your answer reasonable? Why?

_____

_____

CHAPTER 5, Atomic Structure and the Periodic Table *(continued)*

EXTRA PRACTICE (similar to Practice Problem 12, page 117)

12. Three isotopes of sulfur are sulfur-32, sulfur-33, and sulfur-34. Write the complete symbol for each isotope, including the atomic number and the mass number.

sulfur-32 □□S sulfur-33 □□S sulfur-34 □□S

GUIDED PRACTICE PROBLEM 16 (page 121)

16. The element copper has naturally occurring isotopes with mass numbers of 63 and 65. The relative abundance and atomic masses are 69.2% for mass = 62.93 amu and 30.8% for mass = 64.93 amu. Calculate the average atomic mass of copper.

Analyze

Step 1. Will the average atomic mass be closer to 63 or to 65? Explain.

_____

_____

Solve

Step 2. For Cu-63: 69.2% × 62.93 amu = 0.692 × 62.93 amu = [   ]

Step 3. For Cu-65: 30.8% × 64.93 amu = [   ] × [   ] = [   ]

Step 4. Average mass: 43.6 amu + [   ] = [   ]

Evaluate

Step 5. Explain why your answer is reasonable.

_____

EXTRA PRACTICE (similar to Practice Problem 17, page 121)

17. Calculate the atomic mass of rubidium. The two isotopes of rubidium have atomic masses and relative abundancies of 84.91 amu (72.16%) and 86.91 amu (27.84%). _____

6 CHEMICAL NAMES AND FORMULAS

SECTION 6.1 INTRODUCTION TO CHEMICAL BONDING (pages 133–137)

This section explains how to distinguish between ionic and molecular compounds. It also defines cation *and* anion *and relates them to metals and nonmetals.*

▶ Molecules and Molecular Compounds (pages 133–134)

1. All living and nonliving things are made up of building blocks called

   _____ .

2. Most elements found in nature, with the exception of the _____ ,

   exist as molecules.

3. What is a molecule?

   _____

   _____

   _____

4. Compounds that are formed when two or more atoms combine to form

   molecules are called _____ .

5. Circle the letter of the substances that do NOT exist as molecules in nature.

   a. oxygen

   b. water

   c. neon

   d. ozone

   e. helium

6. List three properties of molecular compounds.

   a. _____

   b. _____

   c. _____

© Prentice-Hall, Inc.

CHAPTER 6, Chemical Names and Formulas *(continued)*

▶ Ions and Ionic Compounds *(pages 135–137)*

7. What is an ion?

_____

8. How are ions formed?

_____

9. An atom that gains electrons is called a(n) _____ ; an atom
that loses electrons is called a(n) _____ .

10. Complete the table about anions and cations.

	Anions	**Cations**
Charge		
Metal/Nonmetal		
Name		

11. Give the name and symbol of the ion formed when

a. a calcium atom loses two electrons _____

b. an oxygen atom gains two electrons _____

c. a copper ion loses one electron _____ .

12. Circle the letter of the choice that describes the makeup of an ionic
compound.

a. anions only

b. cations only

c. both anions and cations

13. Explain how compounds made up of ions can be electrically neutral.

_____

14. List three properties of ionic compounds.

a. _____

b. _____

c. _____

SECTION 6.2 REPRESENTING CHEMICAL COMPOUNDS (pages 138–142)

This section explains how to distinguish between two types of chemical formulas—molecular formulas and formula units. It also uses experimental data to demonstrate that a compound obeys the law of definite proportions.

▶ Chemical Formulas (page 138)

1. A chemical formula shows the types and _____ of atoms in the smallest representative unit of a substance.

2. List the numbers and types of atoms represented by these chemical formulas.

    a. Fe_2O_3 _____

    b. $KMnO_4$ _____

    c. CH_4 _____

    d. NH_4NO_3 _____

▶ Molecular Formulas (pages 138–139)

3. What is a molecular formula?

_____

_____

Match each compound with its molecular formula.

_____ **4.** carbon dioxide   **a.** C_2H_6

_____ **5.** ethane   **b.** CO_2

_____ **6.** ammonia   **c.** NH_3

7. Is the following sentence true or false? A molecular formula shows the

    arrangement of the atoms in a molecule. _____

8. Look at Figure 6.5 on page 138. List seven elements that exist as diatomic molecules.

    _____

    _____

    _____

    _____

    _____

    _____

    _____

CHAPTER 6, Chemical Names and Formulas *(continued)*

In the diagram, match the type of model or formula with its representation.

    a. ball-and-stick model

    b. molecular formula

    c. perspective drawing

    d. space-filling molecular model

    e. structural formula

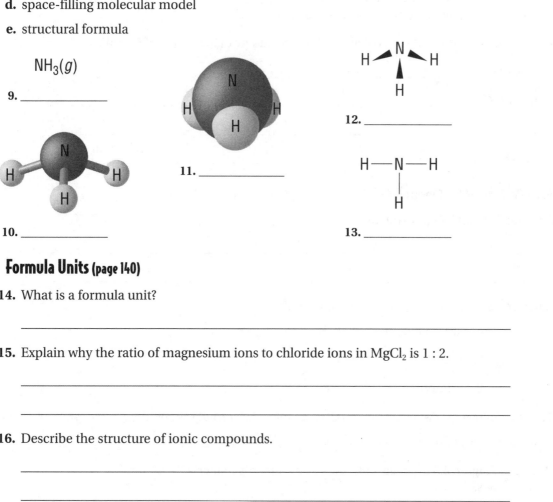

$NH_3(g)$

9. _____

10. _____

11. _____

12. _____

13. _____

▶ Formula Units (page 140)

14. What is a formula unit?

_____

15. Explain why the ratio of magnesium ions to chloride ions in $MgCl_2$ is 1 : 2.

_____

_____

16. Describe the structure of ionic compounds.

_____

_____

_____

▶ The Laws of Definite and Multiple Proportions (pages 141–142)

17. What is the law of definite proportions?

_____

_____

_____

© Prentice-Hall, Inc.

18. Circle the whole-number mass ratio of Li to Cl in LiCl. The atomic mass of Li is 6.9; the atomic mass of Cl is 35.5.

   a. 42 : 1

   b. 5 : 1

   c. 1 : 5

19. Circle the whole-number mass ratio of carbon to hydrogen in C_2H_4. The atomic mass of C is 12.0; the atomic mass of H is 1.0.

   a. 1 : 6

   b. 6 : 1

   c. 1 : 12

   d. 12 : 1

20. In the compound sulfur dioxide, a food preservative, the mass ratio of sulfur to oxygen is 1 : 1. An 80-g sample of a compound composed of sulfur and oxygen contains 48 g of oxygen. Is the sample sulfur dioxide? Explain.

   _____

   _____

21. What is the law of multiple proportions?

   _____

   _____

   _____

22. Complete the table using the law of multiple proportions.

	Mass of Cu	Mass of Cl	Mass Ratio Cl : Cu	Whole-number Ratio of Cl
Compound A	8.3 g	4.6 g		
Compound B	3.3 g	3.6 g		

SECTION 6.3 IONIC CHARGES (pages 143–148)

This section explains the use of the periodic table to determine the charge of an ion. It also defines polyatomic ion *and gives the names and formulas for the most common polyatomic ions.*

▶ Monatomic Ions (pages 143–146)

1. What are monatomic ions?

   _____

CHAPTER 6, Chemical Names and Formulas (continued)

2. How is the ionic charge of a Group 1A, 2A, or 3A ion determined?

_____

3. How is the ionic charge of a Group 5A, 6A, or 7A ion determined?

_____

_____

4. Circle the letter of the type of element that often has more than one common ionic charge.

   a. alkali metal

   b. alkaline earth metal

   c. transition metal

   d. nonmetal

5. The _____ of naming transition metal cations uses a Roman numeral in parentheses to indicate the numeric value of the ionic charge.

6. An older naming system uses the suffix -ous to name the cation with the

   _____ charge, and the suffix -ic to name the cation with the

   _____ charge.

7. What is a major advantage of the Stock system over the old naming system?

_____

8. Use the periodic table to write the name and formula (including charge) for each ion in the table below.

Element	Name	Formula
Fluorine		
Calcium		
Oxygen		

▶ Polyatomic Ions (pages 146–148)

9. What is a polyatomic ion?

_____

_____

© Prentice-Hall, Inc.

10. Is the following sentence true or false? The names of polyatomic anions always end in -*ide*. _____

11. What is the difference between the anions sulfite and sulfate?

_____

12. Look at Table 6.4 on page 147. Circle the letter of a polyatomic ion that is a cation.

    a. ammonium

    b. acetate

    c. oxalate

    d. phosphate

13. How many atoms make up the oxalate ion and what is its charge?

_____

_____

14. What three hydrogen-containing polyatomic anions are essential components of living systems?

    a. _____

    b. _____

    c. _____

15. Look at Figure 6.14 on page 146. Identify each of the ions shown below.

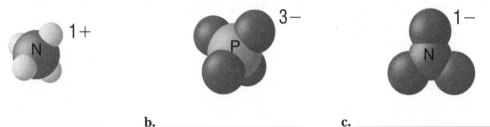

  a. _____   **b.** _____   **c.** _____

SECTION 6.4 IONIC COMPOUNDS (pages 149–156)

This section explains the rules for naming and writing formulas for binary and ternary ionic compounds.

▶ Writing Formulas for Binary Ionic Compounds (pages 149–151)

1. Traditionally, common names were based on some _____ of a compound or its _____ .

2. What is the general name for compounds composed of two elements?

_____

CHAPTER 6, Chemical Names and Formulas *(continued)*

3. When writing the formula for any ionic compound, the charges of the ions

   must _____ .

4. What are two methods for writing a balanced formula?

   a. _____

   b. _____

5. What are the formulas for the compounds formed by the following pairs of ions?

   a. Fe^{2+}, Cl^- _____

   b. Cr^{3+}, O^{2-} _____

   c. Na^+, S^{2-} _____

6. What are the formulas for these compounds?

   a. lithium bromide _____

   b. cupric nitride _____

   c. magnesium chloride _____

▶ Naming Binary Ionic Compounds (pages 151–153)

7. The name of a binary compound is written with the name of the

   _____ first followed by the name of the _____ .

8. How can you tell that cobalt(II) iodide is a binary compound formed by a transition metal with more than one ionic charge?

   _____

   _____

9. Write the names for these binary ionic compounds.

   a. PbS _____

   b. $MgCl_2$ _____

   c. Al_2Se_3 _____

▶ Ternary Ionic Compounds (pages 154–156)

10. What is a ternary compound?

    _____

11. Is the following sentence true or false? Ternary compounds rarely contain

    polyatomic ions. _____

12. Why are parentheses used to write the formula Al(OH)$_3$?

_____

13. Complete the table for these common ternary ionic compounds.

Cation	Anion	Name	Formula
NH$_4^+$	S^{2-}		
Fe^{3+}		iron(III) carbonate	
	NO$_3^-$		AgNO$_3$
		potassium cyanide	KCN

SECTION 6.5 MOLECULAR COMPOUNDS AND ACIDS (pages 158–160)

This section explains the rules for naming and writing formulas for binary molecular compounds. It also briefly describes how to name and write formulas for common acids.

▶ Binary Molecular Compounds (pages 158–159)

1. Circle the letter of the types of elements that form binary molecular compounds.

   a. two nonmetallic elements

   b. a metal and a nonmetal

   c. two metals

2. Is the following sentence true or false? Two nonmetallic elements can combine in only one way. _____

3. What method is used to distinguish between different molecular compounds that contain the same elements? _____

Match the prefix with the number it indicates.

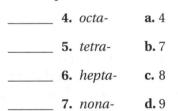

_____ **4.** *octa-*   **a.** 4

_____ **5.** *tetra-*   **b.** 7

_____ **6.** *hepta-*   **c.** 8

_____ **7.** *nona-*   **d.** 9

8. What are the names of the following compounds?

   a. BF$_3$ _____

   b. N$_2$O$_4$ _____

   c. P$_4$S$_7$ _____

© Prentice-Hall, Inc.

CHAPTER 6, Chemical Names and Formulas *(continued)*

9. What are the formulas for the following compounds?

   a. carbon tetrabromide _____

   b. nitrogen triiodide _____

   c. iodine monochloride _____

   d. tetraiodine nonaoxide _____

▶ Naming Common Acids (page 160)

10. Acids produce _____ ions when dissolved in water.

11. When naming acids, you can consider them to be combinations of

    _____ connected to as many _____ ions

    as necessary to create an electrically neutral compound.

12. Use Table 6.4 on page 147 to help you complete the table about acids.

Acid Name	Formula	Anion Name
acetic acid		
carbonic acid		
hydrochloric acid		
nitric acid		
phosphoric acid		
sulfuric acid		

Reading Skill Practice

Writing a summary can help you remember the information you have read. When you write a summary, include only the most important points. Write a summary of the information in Section 6.5 on pages 158–160. Your summary should be shorter than the text on which it is based. Do your work on a separate sheet of paper.

SECTION 6.6 SUMMARY OF NAMING AND FORMULA WRITING (pages 161–163)

This section explains the use of flowcharts to write the name or formula of a compound.

▶ **Practicing Skills: Follow the Arrows** (pages 161–162)

1. How can a flowchart help you to name chemical compounds?

   _____

   _____

2. Use the flowchart in Figure 6.21 on page 161 to write the names of the following compounds:

   a. CsCl _____

   b. $SnSe_2$ _____

   c. NH_4OH _____

   d. HF _____

   e. Si_3N_4 _____

3. Complete the following five rules for writing a chemical formula from a chemical name.

   a. In an ionic compound, the net ionic charge is _____ .

   b. An *-ide* ending generally indicates a _____ compound.

   c. An *-ite* or *-ate* ending means there is a _____ ion that includes oxygen in the formula.

   d. _____ in a name generally indicate that the compound is molecular and show the number of each kind of atom in the molecule.

   e. A _____ after the name of a cation shows the ionic charge of the cation.

4. Look at Figure 6.22 on page 162. Name five metallic elements that are commonly found in the rock formations shown in the photo.

   a. _____

   b. _____

   c. _____

   b. _____

   e. _____

5. What is the indication that these metals are present in rocks?

   _____

CHAPTER 6, Chemical Names and Formulas *(continued)*

6. Fill in the missing labels from Figure 6.23 on page 162.

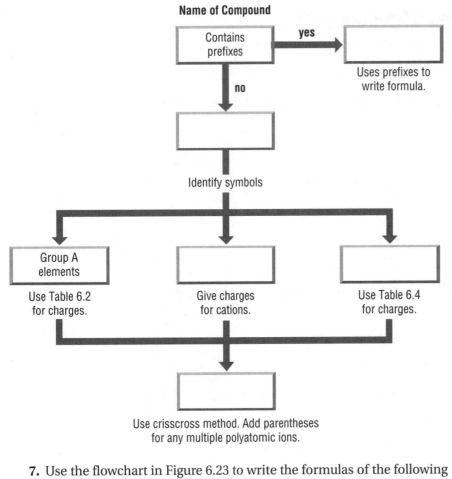

7. Use the flowchart in Figure 6.23 to write the formulas of the following compounds:

   a. potassium silicate _____

   b. phosphorus pentachloride _____

   c. manganese(II) chromate _____

   d. lithium hydride _____

   e. diiodine pentoxide _____

MathWise

GUIDED PRACTICE PROBLEM 10 (page 142)

10. Lead forms two compounds with oxygen. One compound contains 2.98 g of lead combined with 0.461 g of oxygen. The other compound contains 9.89 g of lead with 0.763 g of oxygen. What is the lowest whole-number mass ratio of lead in the two compounds that combines with a given mass of oxygen?

Complete the following steps to solve the problem.

Step 1. Write the ratio of lead to oxygen for each compound.

First compound

$$\frac{\boxed{}\ \text{g lead}}{0.461\ \text{g oxygen}}$$

Second compound

$$\frac{9.89\ \text{g lead}}{\boxed{}\ \text{g oxygen}}$$

Step 2. Divide the numerator by the denominator in each ratio.

$$\frac{6.46\ \boxed{}}{\boxed{}}$$

$$\frac{\boxed{}\ \text{g lead}}{\text{g oxygen}}$$

Step 3. Write a ratio comparing the first compound to the second.

$$\frac{\boxed{}\ \text{g lead/g oxygen}}{13.0\ \text{g lead/g oxygen}}$$

Step 4. Simplify. Note that this ratio has no units.

$$\frac{0.497}{1} = \text{roughly}\ \frac{1}{\boxed{}}$$

The mass ratio of lead per gram of oxygen in the two compounds is _____ .

GUIDED PRACTICE PROBLEMS 24B AND 24C (page 151)

24. Write formulas for compounds formed from these pairs of ions.

b. Li^+, O^{2-}

Analyze

Step 1. Do the ions combine in a one-to-one ratio? How do you know?

_____

Solve

Step 2. Use the crisscross method to balance the formula.

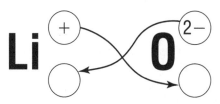

CHAPTER 6, Chemical Names and Formulas *(continued)*

Evaluate

Step 3. How do you know your formula is reasonable?

_____

_____

c. Ca^{2+}, N^{3-}

Analyze

Step 1. Will the calcium (Ca^{2+}) and nitride (N^{3-}) ions combine in a 1 : 1 ratio? How do you know?

_____

_____

Solve

Step 2. Use the crisscross method to balance the formula.

$$Ca^{2+} \quad N^{3-}$$

Evaluate

Step 3. How do you know this formula is reasonable?

_____

_____

GUIDED PRACTICE PROBLEMS 26 *(page 153)*

26. Write the names for these ionic binary compounds.

    a. ZnS   **c.** BaO

Use the flowchart in Figure 6.21, page 161, to help you. Answer each question to find which path to take to the next question.

  a. FeS

- How do you know that the answer to the first question in the flowchart is *no*?

_____

- How do you know that the answer to the second question in the flowchart is *no*?

_____

- Based on this answer, what suffix will be at the end of the compound name?

_____

© Prentice-Hall, Inc.

- Is Fe a metal? _____ Is it a Group A element? _____
- What is the name of the element Fe? _____ Of the element S? _____
- What Roman numeral belongs with the cation? How do you know?

  _____

- Name the compound FeS. _____

c. BaO

- What element is O? _____What element is Ba? _____
- How does the name of this compound end? _____
- Is Ba a metal? _____ Is it a Group A metal? _____
- Name the compound BaO. _____

GUIDED PRACTICE PROBLEM 29 (page 155)

29. Write the formula for chromium(III) nitrate.

- Is the compound ionic or molecular? Explain.

  _____

- Use Table 6.4 on page 147 to write the formula for the nitrate ion. _____
- Use the crisscross method to balance the formula.
- Write the formula. _____

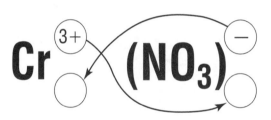

GUIDED PRACTICE PROBLEM 31b (page 155)

31. Write the name for the compound $NaClO_3$.

Use the flowchart in Figure 6.21 on page 161 to help you.

- Is the first element hydrogen? What does this tell you?

  _____

- Does the formula contain more than two elements? What does this tell you?

  _____

- Is sodium a Group A metal? What does this tell you about the name of the first ion in the compound?

  _____

- Use Table 6.4 on page 147 to find the name of the anion. Write the name of the compound. _____

7 CHEMICAL QUANTITIES

SECTION 7.1 THE MOLE: A MEASUREMENT OF MATTER (pages 171–180)

This section explains how Avogadro's number is related to a mole of any substance. It teaches you how to calculate the mass of a mole of any substance.

▶ What Is a Mole? (pages 171–173)

1. What do the questions "how much?" and "how many?" have in common?

   _____

2. List two or three ways to measure matter.

   _____

3. Circle the letter of the term that is an SI unit for measuring the amount of a substance.

   a. dozen   **b.** ounce   **c.** pair   **d.** mole

▶ The Number of Particles in a Mole (pages 173–176)

4. What is Avogadro's number?

   _____

5. Circle the letter of the term that is NOT a representative particle of a substance.

   a. molecule   **b.** atom   **c.** grain   **d.** formula unit

6. List the representative particle for each of the following types of substances.

   a. molecular compounds   _____

   b. ionic compounds   _____

   c. elements   _____

7. Is the following sentence true or false? To determine the number of
   representative particles in a compound, you count the molecules by viewing
   them under a microscope. _____

8. How can you determine the number of atoms in a mole of a molecular compound?

   _____

   _____

   _____

© Prentice-Hall, Inc.

CHAPTER 7, Chemical Quantities *(continued)*

9. Complete the table about representative particles and moles.

Representative Particles and Moles			
	Representative Particle	**Chemical Formula**	**Representative Particles in 1.00 mol**
Atomic oxygen		O	
Oxygen gas	Molecule		
Sodium ion			
Sodium chloride			

▶ The Mass of a Mole of an Element (pages 176–178)

10. What is the gram atomic mass (gam)?

_____

11. Circle the letter of the phrase that completes this sentence correctly. The gram atomic masses of any two elements must contain

    a. the same number of molecules.

    b. the same number of atoms.

    c. the same number of formula units.

▶ The Mass of a Mole of a Compound (pages 178–181)

12. How do you determine the mass of a mole of a molecular compound?

_____

_____

_____

13. Complete the labels on the diagram below.

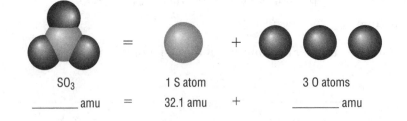

SO_3 1 S atom   3 O atoms

_____ amu   =   32.1 amu   +   _____ amu

14. What is the gram molecular mass (gmm) of a compound?

_____

_____

15. Is the following sentence true or false? Gram molecular masses can be calculated directly from gram atomic masses. _____

16. What is the gram formula mass (gfm) of a compound?

_____

_____

SECTION 7.2   MOLE-MASS AND MOLE-VOLUME RELATIONSHIPS (pages 182–187)

This section explains how to use molar mass to convert among measurements of mass, volume, and number of particles.

▶ The Molar Mass of a Substance (pages 182–183)

1. What is the molar mass of a substance?

_____

_____

2. What is the molar mass of KI (potassium iodide)?

_____

_____

▶ The Volume of a Mole of Gas (pages 184–185)

3. Is the following sentence true or false? The volumes of one mole of different solid and liquid substances are the same. _____

4. Circle the letter of each term that can complete this sentence correctly. The volume of a gas varies with a change in

    a. temperature.   **c.** pressure.

    b. the size of the container.   **d.** the amount of light in the container.

5. Circle the letter of the temperature that is defined as standard temperature.

    a. 0 K   **c.** 0 °C

    b. 100 K   **d.** 100 °C

6. Is the following sentence true or false? Standard pressure is 101.3 kPa or 1 atmosphere (atm). _____

7. What is the molar volume of a gas at standard temperature and pressure (STP)? _____

8. What units do you normally use to describe the density of a gas?

_____

© Prentice-Hall, Inc.

CHAPTER 7, Chemical Quantities *(continued)*

▶ **The Mole Road Map** (page 185)

9. The figure below shows how to convert from one unit to another unit. Write the missing conversion factors below.

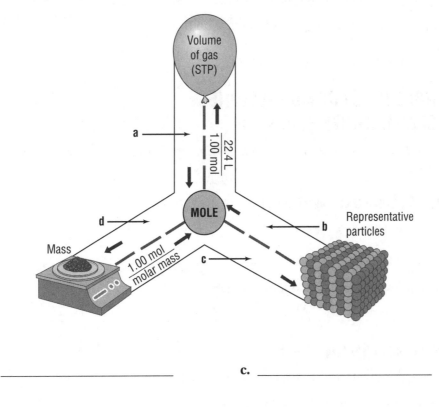

a. _____

b. _____

c. _____

d. _____

SECTION 7.3 PERCENT COMPOSITION AND CHEMICAL FORMULAS (pages 188–195)

This section explains how to calculate percent composition from chemical formulas or experimental data, and how to derive empirical and molecular formulas.

▶ **Calculating the Percent Composition of a Compound** (pages 188–191)

1. How do you express relative amounts of each element in a compound?

_____

2. Circle the letter of the phrase that completes this sentence correctly. The number of percent values in the percent composition of a compound is

   a. half as many as there are different elements in the compound.

   b. as many as there are different elements in the compound.

   c. twice as many as there are different elements in the compound.

© Prentice-Hall, Inc.

3. What is the formula for the percent by mass of an element in a compound?

_____

4. In the diagram below, which compound has a greater percent composition of chromium? _____

How much greater is this percent? _____

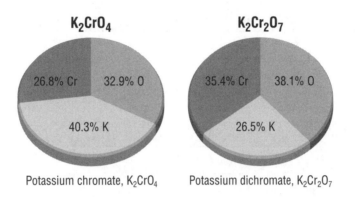

K₂CrO₄

K₂Cr₂O₇

Potassium chromate, K₂CrO₄   Potassium dichromate, K₂Cr₂O₇

5. To calculate the percent composition of a known compound, start with the chemical formula of the compound and calculate the _____ , which gives the mass of one mole of the compound.

▶ Using Percent as a Conversion Factor (pages 191–192)

6. Is the following sentence true or false? You can use percent composition to calculate the number of grams of an element in a given amount of a compound. _____

7. How do you calculate the grams of an element in a specific amount of a compound?

_____

_____

▶ Calculating Empirical Formulas (pages 192–193)

8. An empirical formula of a compound gives the _____ whole-number ratio of the atoms of the elements in a compound.

9. Is the following sentence true or false? The empirical formula of a compound is always the same as the molecular formula. _____

10. Look at Figure 7.18 and Table 7.2. Name three compounds that have an empirical formula of CH.

_____

© Prentice-Hall, Inc.

CHAPTER 7, Chemical Quantities *(continued)*

11. Fill in the labels on the diagram below.

SO$_3$ molecule   composed of   _____ S atom   and   3 _____ atoms

MICROSCOPIC INTERPRETATION

SO$_3$

MACROSCOPIC INTERPRETATION

1 mol SO$_3$ composed of   _____ sulfur atoms

and

_____ × (_____ × 10^{23}) oxygen atoms

▶ Calculating Molecular Formulas (page 194)

12. The molecular formula of a compound is either the same as its empirical

formula or a _____ of it.

13. What do you need to know to calculate the molecular formula of a compound?

_____

14. If you divide the molar mass of a compound by the empirical formula mass, what is the result?

_____

15. What would you use to convert the empirical formula of a compound to a molecular formula?

_____

📖 Reading Skill Practice

By looking carefully at photographs and illustrations in textbooks, you can better understand what you have read. Look carefully at Figure 7.17 on page 192. What important idea does this illustration communicate?

MathWise

GUIDED PRACTICE PROBLEM 3 (page 174)

3. How many moles is 2.80×10^{24} atoms of silicon?

Step 1. List what you know.

2.80×10^{24} atoms of Si

[ ] atoms in one mole

Step 2. Multiply the atoms of silicon by a mol/atoms conversion factor.

2.80×10^{24} atoms Si $\times \dfrac{1 \text{ mol}}{\boxed{} \text{ atoms Si}}$

Step 3. Simplify the factors.

$\dfrac{\boxed{} \text{mol}}{6.02}$

Step 4. Divide.

[ ] mol

GUIDED PRACTICE PROBLEM 7C (page 179)

7C. Find the gram molecular mass of C_3H_7OH.

Step 1. List the knowns and the unknown.

Known	Unknown
molecular formula: C_3H_7OH	gmm = ?

1 gam C = [ ]

1 gam H = [ ]

1 gam O = [ ]

Step 2. List the moles of each element in one mole of the compound.

3 mol C, from C_3

_____ mol H, from H_7 and H

_____ mol O, from O

Step 3. Multiply the numbers of moles by each mass/mol conversion factor.

$3 \cancel{\text{ mol C}} \times \dfrac{12.0 \text{ g}}{\cancel{\text{mol}}} = \boxed{} \text{ g}$

$8 \cancel{\text{ mol H}} \times \dfrac{\boxed{} \text{ g}}{\cancel{\text{mol}}} = 8.0 \text{ g}$

$\boxed{} \cancel{\text{ mol O}} \times \dfrac{\boxed{} \text{ g}}{\cancel{\text{mol}}} = \boxed{}$

Step 4. Add the masses of the three elements.

$\text{gmm} = 36.0 \text{ g} + \boxed{} + 16.0 \text{ g} = \boxed{}$

CHAPTER 7, Chemical Quantities *(continued)*

EXTRA PRACTICE (similar to Practice Problem 5, page 175)

5. How many atoms are there in 2.00 moles of SO_3?

EXTRA PRACTICE (similar to Practice Problem 8, page 179)

8. What is the mass of 1 mole of ozone (O_3)?

EXTRA PRACTICE (similar to Practice Problem 10, page 181)

10. Find the gram formula mass of table salt (sodium chloride).

EXTRA PRACTICE (similar to Practice Problem 17, page 183)

17. Calculate the mass, in grams, of 10 mol of sodium sulfate (Na_2SO_4).

Calculate the mass, in grams, of 10 mol of iron(II) hydroxide ($Fe(OH)_2$).

GUIDED PRACTICE PROBLEM 18 (page 183)

18. Find the number of moles in each quantity.

a. 3.70×10^{-1} g B   **c.** 847 g $(NH_4)_2CO_3$

Analyze

Step 1. List the knowns and unknowns.

3.70×10^{-1} g B

1 gam B = 10.8 g

number of moles = ?

847 g $(NH_4)_2CO_3$

1 gam N = 14.0 g

1 gam H = ☐ g

1 gam ☐ = 12.0 g

1 gam O = ☐

number of moles = ?

Step 2. Add the atomic masses to find the molar mass of the compound, if necessary.

gfm = 2 mol N + 8 mol H
    + 1 mol C + 3 mol O

= ☐ g + 8.0 g + ☐ + 48 g

= ☐ g

Solve

Step 3. Multiply the given quantity by a mass/ mol conversion factor.

3.70×10^{-1} g̶ ̶B̶ $\times \dfrac{1 \text{ mol}}{\boxed{}}$

= ☐ mol B

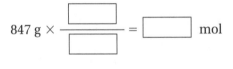

847 g $\times$ ☐ = ☐ mol

Evaluate

Step 4. Is the answer reasonable?

Because 3.70 g is about one third the atomic mass of boron the (10.8 amu), the answer should be about one third mole, times a factor of 10^{-1}, and it is.

Because 847 g is 8 or 9 times the gfm of the compound, answer should be between 8 or 9 moles, which it is.

EXTRA PRACTICE (similar to Practice Problem 33, page 191)

33. Calculate the mass of hydrogen in these compounds.

a. 200 g ethane (20% hydrogen by mass)

b. 50.0 g ammonium chloride (about 7.5% H)

CHEMICAL REACTIONS

SECTION 8.1 DESCRIBING CHEMICAL CHANGE (pages 203–211)

This section explains how to write equations describing chemical reactions using appropriate symbols. It also describes how to write balanced chemical equations when given the names or formulas of the reactants and products in a chemical reaction.

▶ Word Equations (pages 203–204)

1. A chemical reaction occurs when one or more _____ change into one or more new substances, or _____ .

2. The arrow in a reaction means _____

_____ .

3. What is the law of conservation of mass?

_____

4. Is the following sentence true or false? When there are two or more reactants or products, they are separated by an arrow. _____

5. Write a word equation that describes the following reactions.

   a. Acetylene reacts with oxygen to produce carbon dioxide and water.

   _____

   b. When heated, mercury(II) oxide reacts to form mercury and oxygen.

   _____

▶ Chemical Equations (pages 205–206)

6. What is a chemical equation?

_____

_____

7. A chemical reaction that shows only the formulas, but not the relative amounts of the reactants and products is a(n) _____ .

8. Identify the reactant(s) and product(s) in the chemical equation
   $Li + Br_2 \longrightarrow LiBr$.

   a. reactant(s) _____

   b. product(s) _____

CHAPTER 8, Chemical Reactions *(continued)*

9. Circle the letter of each statement that is true about a catalyst.

    a. A catalyst is the new material produced as a result of a chemical reaction.

    b. A catalyst is not used up in a chemical reaction.

    c. A catalyst adds heat to a chemical reaction.

    d. A catalyst speeds up a chemical reaction.

10. Use the symbols in Table 8.1 on page 206 to write a skeleton equation for the following chemical reaction. Hydrochloric acid reacts with zinc to produce aqueous zinc(II) chloride and hydrogen gas.

_____

▶ Balancing Chemical Equations (pages 207–211)

11. Complete the flowchart for balancing equations.

Determine the correct formulas and physical states for

the _____ and _____ .

↓

Write a _____ with the reactants on the

left and the products on the right of a yields sign (⟶).

↓

Count the number of _____ of each

element in the reactants and products.

↓

Balance the elements by using _____

in front of formulas. Never try to balance an equation

by changing the _____ in formulas.

↓

Check each atom or polyatomic ion to be sure the equation

is _____ , and make sure that all coefficients

are in the _____ possible ratio.

12. Balance the following chemical equations.

a. _____ Na(*s*) + _____ H$_2$O(*l*) ⟶ _____ NaOH(*aq*) + H$_2$(*g*)

b. _____ AgNO$_3$(*aq*) + Zn(*s*) ⟶ Zn(NO$_3$)$_2$(*aq*) + _____ Ag(*s*)

SECTION 8.2 TYPES OF CHEMICAL REACTIONS (pages 212–224)

This section explains how to identify a reaction as a combination, decomposition, single-replacement, double-replacement, or combustion reaction. It also describes how to predict the products of each type of reaction.

▶ Chemical Reactions (page 212)

1. There are _____ types of chemical reactions.

▶ Combination Reactions (pages 212–214)

2. Complete the diagram of a combination reaction. Which characteristics of this type of reaction are shown in the diagram?

_____

_____

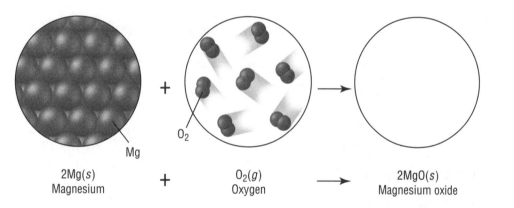

| 2Mg(*s*) | + | O$_2$(*g*) | ⟶ | 2MgO(*s*) |
| Magnesium | | Oxygen | | Magnesium oxide |

3. Is the following sentence true or false? The product of a combination reaction is always a molecular compound. _____

4. Circle the letter of each set of reactants that can produce more than one product.

a. two nonmetals   **c.** a transition metal and a nonmetal

b. a Group A metal and a nonmetal   **d.** two metals

▶ Decomposition Reactions (pages 214–216)

5. Look at Figure 8.6 on page 215. Which characteristics of a decomposition reaction are shown in the diagram?

_____

_____

CHAPTER 8, Chemical Reactions *(continued)*

6. Rapid decomposition reactions can cause _____ as a result of the formation of gaseous products and heat.

7. Most decomposition reactions require the addition of _____ in the form of heat, light, or electricity.

▶ Single-Replacement Reactions *(pages 216–218)*

8. Complete the diagram of a single replacement reaction. Which characteristics of this type of reaction are shown in the diagram?

_____

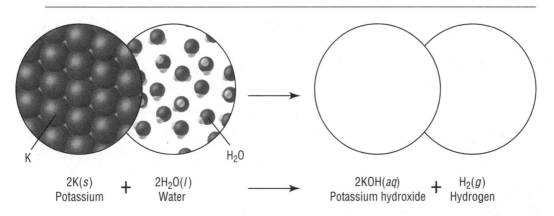

2K(*s*)	+	2H₂O(*l*)		2KOH(*aq*)	+	H₂(*g*)

$2K(s)$ + $2H_2O(l)$ ⟶ $2KOH(aq)$ + $H_2(g)$
Potassium + Water ⟶ Potassium hydroxide + Hydrogen

9. Using Table 8.2 on page 217, state whether the following combinations will produce a reaction or no reaction.

   a. $Ag(s)$ + $HCl(aq)$ _____

   b. $Cu(s)$ + $AgNO_3(aq)$ _____

▶ Double-Replacement Reactions *(pages 218–220)*

10. Look at Figure 8.10 on page 219. Which characteristics of a double-replacement reaction are shown in the diagram?

_____

_____

_____

11. When solutions of ionic compounds are mixed, what three circumstances indicate that a double-replacement reaction has occurred?

   a. _____

   b. _____

   c. _____

▶ Combustion Reactions (pages 220–221)

12. Look at the diagram of a combustion reaction in Figure 8.11 on page 221. Which characteristics of this type of reaction are shown in the diagram?

_____

13. Is the following sentence true or false? Hydrocarbons, compounds of hydrogen and carbon, are often the reactants in combustion reactions. _____

14. Circle the letter of each compound that can be produced by combustion reactions.

   a. oxygen   **c.** water

   b. carbon dioxide   **d.** glucose

▶ Predicting Products of a Chemical Reaction (pages 222–224)

15. Classify the reaction in each of the following equations.

   a. $BaCl_2(aq) + K_2CrO_4(aq) \longrightarrow BaCrO_4(s) + 2KCl\ (aq)$ _____

   b. $Si(s) + 2Cl_2(g) \longrightarrow SiCl_4(l)$ _____

   c. $2C_6H_6(l) + 15O_2(g) \longrightarrow 6H_2O(l) + 12CO_2(g)$ _____

16. Use Figure 8.12 on page 223. The equation for the combustion of pentane is $C_5H_{12} + 8O_2 \longrightarrow 5CO_2 + 6H_2O$. What numbers in this equation are represented by x and y in the general equation? _____

SECTION 8.3 REACTIONS IN AQUEOUS SOLUTIONS (pages 225–228)

This section explains how to write and balance net ionic equations. It also describes the use of solubility rules to predict the precipitate formed in double-replacement reactions.

▶ Net Ionic Equations (pages 225–227)

1. Many important chemical reactions take place in _____ .

2. An equation that shows dissolved ionic compounds as their free ions is called a(n) _____ .

3. Is the following sentence true or false? A spectator ion is not directly involved in a reaction. _____

4. What is a net ionic equation? _____

_____

_____

© Prentice-Hall, Inc.

CHAPTER 8, Chemical Reactions *(continued)*

5. Circle the letter of each sentence that is true about ionic equations.

    a. A complete ionic equation shows only the ions involved in the reaction.

    b. Spectator ions can be left out of a net ionic equation.

    c. Atoms do not need to be balanced in an ionic equation.

    d. Ionic charges must be balanced in a net ionic equation.

6. Write the balanced net ionic equation for this reaction:
    $Pb(NO_3)_2(aq) + KI(aq) \longrightarrow PbI_2(s) + KNO_3(aq)$. Show your work.

    _____

    _____

    _____

    _____

▶ Predicting the Formation of a Precipitate (pages 227–228)

7. What determines whether a precipitate forms when two solutions of ionic compounds are mixed?

    _____

8. Use Table 8.3 on page 227 to predict whether the following compounds will be soluble or insoluble.

    a. $Fe(OH)_3$ _____

    b. NaOH _____

    c. $Ca(ClO_3)_2$ _____

    d. $HgSO_4$ _____

📖 Reading Skill Practice

A flowchart can help you to remember the order in which events occur. On a separate sheet of paper, create a flowchart that describes the steps for writing a balanced net ionic equation. This process is explained on pages 225–226 of your textbook.

MathWise

GUIDED PRACTICE PROBLEM 3c (page 209)

3c. Balance this equation: $Zn(OH)_2 + H_3PO_4 \longrightarrow Zn_3(PO_4)_2 + H_2O$

Step 1. Look at the zinc ions on both sides of the equation. Make the number of zinc ions in zinc hydroxide match the number in zinc phosphate.

_____ $Zn(OH)_2 + H_3PO_4 \longrightarrow Zn_3(PO_4)_2 + H_2O$

Step 2. Look at the phosphate ions on both sides of the equation. Make the number of phosphate ions in phosphoric acid match the number of phosphate ions in zinc phosphate.

$3Zn(OH)_2 + $ _____ $H_3PO_4 \longrightarrow Zn_3(PO_4)_2 + H_2O$

Step 3. Look at the remaining ions in the reactants—OH^- and H^+.

$3 \times$ _____ ions of OH^-

$2 \times$ _____ ions of H^+ $\longrightarrow$ will form _____ molecules of H_2O

Step 4. Complete the balanced equation.

_____ $Zn(OH)_2 + $ _____ $H_3PO_4 \longrightarrow Zn_3(PO_4)_2 + $ _____ H_2O

GUIDED PRACTICE PROBLEM 13a (page 214)

13a. Complete and balance this combination reaction: $Be + O_2 \longrightarrow$

Step 1. Check the ionic charges of beryllium and oxygen to find the ratio in which they will combine.	The Be ion has a charge of $2+$. The O ion has a charge of $2-$. Be and O will combine to form. _____
Step 2. Begin balancing the equation by looking at oxygen. Multiply the product by a coefficient that will balance the oxygen ions and atoms on both sides of the equation.	$Be + O_2 \longrightarrow$ _____ BeO
Step 3. Find how many beryllium atoms are needed.	_____ $Be + O_2 \longrightarrow 2BeO$

CHAPTER 8, Chemical Reactions *(continued)*

GUIDED PRACTICE PROBLEM 15b (page 216)

15b. Complete and balance this decomposition reaction: $Mg(ClO_3)_2 \longrightarrow MgCl_2 + ?$

Step 1. Determine the second product and write the skeleton equation. Because oxygen atoms are in the reactant, they must also be in a product.	$Mg(ClO_3)_2 \longrightarrow MgCl_2 + \underline{\hspace{1cm}}$
Step 2. Balance the number of oxygen atoms on both sides of the equation.	$Mg(ClO_3)_2 \longrightarrow MgCl_2 + \underline{\hspace{1cm}} O_2$

GUIDED PRACTICE PROBLEM 19b (page 220)

19b. Write a balanced equation for this double-replacement reaction:
$H_2SO_4 + Al(OH)_3 \longrightarrow$

Step 1. Determine the products and write the skeleton equation. One product is water and one is a precipitate.	$H_2SO_4 + Al(OH)_3 \longrightarrow$ $\underline{\hspace{2cm}} + H_2O$
Step 2. Begin balancing the equation. First balance the aluminum.	$\underline{\hspace{0.6cm}} H_2SO_4 + \underline{\hspace{0.6cm}} Al(OH)_3 \longrightarrow$ $\underline{\hspace{0.6cm}} Al_2(SO_4)_3 + H_2O$
Step 3. Then balance the sulfate ions.	$\underline{\hspace{0.6cm}} H_2SO_4 + 2Al(OH)_3 \longrightarrow$ $Al_2(SO_4)_3 + H_2O$
Step 4. Complete the balanced equation.	$3H_2SO_4 + 2Al(OH)_3 \longrightarrow$ $Al_2(SO_4)_3 + \underline{\hspace{0.6cm}} H_2O$

GUIDED PRACTICE PROBLEM 27 (page 228)

27. Write a complete ionic equation and a net ionic equation for the reaction of aqueous solutions of iron(III) nitrate and sodium hydroxide.

Step 1. List the ionic charges of the reactants.	$Fe^{\square} + NO_3^- + Na^{\square} + OH^{\square}$
Step 2. Determine which ions will form a precipitate. Write the complete ionic equation.	$Fe^{3+} + NO_3^- + Na^+ + OH^- \longrightarrow$ $Fe(OH)_3(s) + \underline{\hspace{1.5cm}} + \underline{\hspace{1.5cm}}$
Step 3. Remove the spectator ions to write a net ionic equation.	$Fe^{3+} + OH^- \longrightarrow \underline{\hspace{1.5cm}}$
Step 4. Balance the net ionic equation.	$Fe^{3+} + \underline{\hspace{0.8cm}} OH^- \longrightarrow Fe(OH)_3 (s)$

9 STOICHIOMETRY

SECTION 9.1 THE ARITHMETIC OF EQUATIONS (pages 237–241)

This section explains how to calculate the amount of reactants required or product formed in a non-chemical process. It teaches you how to interpret chemical equations in terms of interacting moles, representative particles, masses, and gas volume at STP.

▶ Using Everyday Equations (pages 237–238)

1. How can you determine the quantities of reactants and products in a chemical reaction?

   _____

   _____

2. Quantity usually means the _____ of a substance expressed in grams or moles.

3. Is the following sentence true or false? Stoichiometry is the calculation of

   quantities in chemical reactions. _____

4. A bookcase is to be built from 3 shelves (Sh), 2 side boards (Sb), 1 top (T), 1 base (B), and 4 legs (L). Write a "balanced equation" for the construction of this bookcase.

   _____

▶ Interpreting Chemical Equations (pages 239–241)

5. From what elements is ammonia produced? How is it used?

   _____

   _____

6. Circle the letter of the term that tells what kind of information you CANNOT get from a chemical equation.

   a. moles

   b. mass

   c. size of particles

   d. volume

   e. number of particles

CHAPTER 9, Stoichiometry *(continued)*

7. The coefficients of a balanced chemical equation tell you the relative number

of moles of _____ and _____ in a

chemical reaction.

8. Why is the relative number of moles of reactants and products the most important information that a balanced chemical equation provides?

_____

_____

9. Is the following sentence true or false? A balanced chemical equation must

obey the law of conservation of mass. _____

10. Use Figure 9.4 on page 239. Complete the table about the reaction of nitrogen and hydrogen.

$N_2(g)$	$+$ $3H_2(g)$	$\rightarrow$ $2NH_3(g)$
[ ] atoms N	$+$ 6 atoms H	$\rightarrow$ [ ] atoms N and [ ] atoms H
1 molecule N_2	$+$ [ ] molecules H_2	$\rightarrow$ [ ] molecules NH_3
[ ] $\times$ (6.02 $\times$ 10^{23} molecules N_2)	$+$ 3 $\times$ (6.02 $\times$ 10^{23} molecules H_2)	$\rightarrow$ [ ] $\times$ (6.02 $\times$ 10^{23} molecules NH_3)
1 mol N_2	$+$ [ ] mol H_2	$\rightarrow$ 2 mol NH_3
28 g N_2	$+$ 3 $\times$ [ ] g H_2	$\rightarrow$ 2 $\times$ [ ] g NH_3
	[ ] g reactants	$\rightarrow$ 34 g products
Assume STP 22.4 L N_2	$+$ 67.2 L H_2	$\rightarrow$ [ ] L NH_3

11. Circle the letter(s) of the items that are ALWAYS conserved in every chemical reaction.

a. volume of gases   **d.** moles

b. mass   **e.** molecules

c. formula units   **f.** atoms

12. What reactant combines with oxygen to form sulfur dioxide? Where can this reactant be found in nature?

_____

_____

SECTION 9.2 CHEMICAL CALCULATIONS (pages 242–250)

This section shows you how to construct mole ratios from balanced chemical equations. It then teaches you how to calculate stoichiometric quantities from balanced chemical equations using units of moles, mass, representative particles, and volumes of gases at STP.

▶ Mole-Mole Calculations (pages 242–244)

1. What is essential for all calculations involving amounts of reactants and

   products? _____

2. Is the following sentence true or false? If you know the number of moles
   of one substance in a reaction, you need more information than the
   balanced chemical equation to determine the number of moles of all the
   other substances in the reaction.

   _____

3. The coefficients from a balanced chemical equation are used to write

   conversion factors called _____ .

4. What are mole ratios used for?

   _____

   _____

   _____

   _____

5. The equation for the formation of potassium chloride is given by the equation

   $2K(s) + Cl_2(g) \longrightarrow 2KCl(s)$

   Write the six possible mole ratios for this equation.

   _____   _____

   _____   _____

   _____   _____

▶ Mass-Mass Calculations (pages 244–247)

6. Is the following sentence true or false? Laboratory balances are used to

   measure moles of substances directly. _____

7. The amount of a substance is *usually* determined by measuring its mass

   in _____ .

CHAPTER 9, Stoichiometry *(continued)*

8. Is the following sentence true or false? If a sample is measured in grams, molar

mass can be used to convert the mass to moles. _____

9. Complete the flow chart to show the steps for the mass–mass conversion of
any given mass of *G* to any wanted mass of *W*. In the chemical equation, *a*
moles of *G* react with *b* moles of *W*.

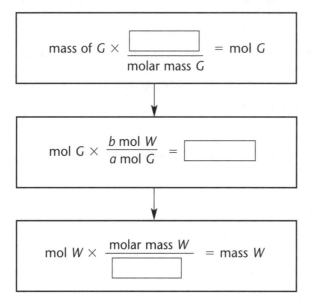

10. Use the diagram below. Describe the steps needed to solve a mass–mass
stoichiometry problem.

_____

_____

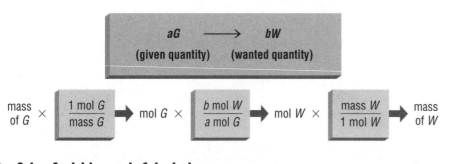

▶ Other Stoichiometric Calculations (pages 247–250)

11. Is the following sentence true or false? Stoichiometric calculations can be
expanded to include any unit of measurement that is related to the mole.

_____

12. List two or three types of problems that can be solved with stoichiometric calculations. _____

_____

13. In any problem relating to stoichiometric calculations, the given quantity is first converted to _____ .

14. The combustion of methane produces carbon dioxide and water. The chemical equation for this reaction is

$$CH_4(g) + 2O_2(g) \longrightarrow CO_2(g) + 2H_2O(g)$$

Write the three conversion factors you would use to find the volume of carbon dioxide obtained from 1.5 L of oxygen.

_____ _____ _____

Reading Skill Practice

Sometimes information you read is easier to remember if you write it in a different format. For example, the paragraph on page 247 and Figure 9.10 both explain how to solve stoichiometric problems. Use these explanations to make a diagram or flow chart for solving a particle–mass stoichiometry problem. Do your work on a separate sheet of paper.

SECTION 9.3 LIMITING REAGENT AND PERCENT YIELD (pages 252–256)

This section helps you identify and use the limiting reagent in a reaction to calculate the maximum amount of product(s) produced and the amount of excess reagent. It also explains how to calculate theoretical yield, actual yield, or percent yield, given appropriate information.

▶ What Is a Limiting Reagent? (pages 252–256)

1. What is a limiting reagent? _____

_____

2. Is the following sentence true or false? A chemical reaction stops before the limiting reagent is used up. _____

3. Circle the letter of the term that correctly completes the sentence. The reactant that is not completely used up in a chemical reaction is called the _____ .

    a. spectator reagent   **c.** excess reagent

    b. limiting reagent   **d.** catalyst

CHAPTER 9, Stoichiometry *(continued)*

4. If the quantities of reactants are given in units other than moles, what is the first step for determining the amount of product?

   a. Determine the amount of product from the given amount of limiting reagent.

   b. Convert each given quantity of reactant to moles.

   c. Identify the limiting reagent.

5. In the diagram below, which reactant is the limiting reagent and why? The chemical equation for the formation of water is $2H_2 + O_2 \longrightarrow 2H_2O$.

   _____

   _____

Experimental Conditions		
Reactants		Products
2 molecules O_2	3 molecules H_2	0 molecules H_2O

Before reaction

▶ Calculating the Percent Yield *(pages 256–258)*

6. What is the theoretical yield?

   _____

   _____

7. The amount of product that actually forms when a chemical reaction is carried out in a laboratory is called the _____ yield.

8. Is the following sentence true or false? The actual yield is usually greater than the theoretical yield. _____

9. Complete the equation for the percent yield of a chemical reaction.

$$\text{Percent yield} = \frac{\boxed{} \text{ yield}}{\boxed{} \text{ yield}} \times 100\%$$

10. Describe four factors that may cause percent yields to be less than 100%.

    _____

    _____

© Prentice-Hall, Inc.

GUIDED PRACTICE PROBLEM 10 (page 244)

10. This equation shows the formation of aluminum oxide.

$$4Al(s) + 3O_2(g) \longrightarrow 2Al_2O_3(s)$$

a. How many moles of oxygen are required to react completely with 14.8 moles of aluminum?

Analyze

1. What is the given information? _____

2. What is the unknown? _____

3. What conversion factor will you need to use? _____

Solve

4. Complete the solution. 14.8 _____ $\times \dfrac{3 \text{ mol } O_2}{\boxed{}}$ = _____ mol O_2

Evaluate

5. Why does the answer have three significant figures?

_____

_____

_____

b. How many moles of aluminum oxide are formed when 0.78 moles of oxygen react with an excess of aluminum?

Analyze

6. What information is given? _____

7. What information is unknown? _____

Solve

8. Complete the solution. _____ mol O_2 $\times \dfrac{\boxed{} \text{ mol } Al_2O_3}{\boxed{}}$

= _____ mol Al_2O_3

Evaluate

9. Why does the answer have two significant figures?

_____

_____

CHAPTER 9, Stoichiometry *(continued)*

EXTRA PRACTICE (similar to Practice Problem 13, page 248)

13. How many molecules of oxygen are produced by the decomposition of 1225 grams of potassium chlorate ($KClO_3$)?

$$2KClO_3(s) \longrightarrow 2KCl(s) + 3O_2(g)$$

EXTRA PRACTICE (similar to Practice Problem 15, page 249)

15. The equation for the combustion of carbon monoxide is

$$2CO(g) + O_2(g) \longrightarrow 2CO_2(g)$$

How many liters of oxygen are needed to burn 10 liters of carbon monoxide?

GUIDED PRACTICE PROBLEM 23 (page 254)

23. The equation for the complete combustion of ethene (C_2H_4) is

$$C_2H_4(g) + 3O_2(g) \longrightarrow 2CO_2(g) + 2H_2O(g)$$

a. If 2.70 moles of ethene reacted with 6.30 moles of oxygen, identify the limiting reagent.

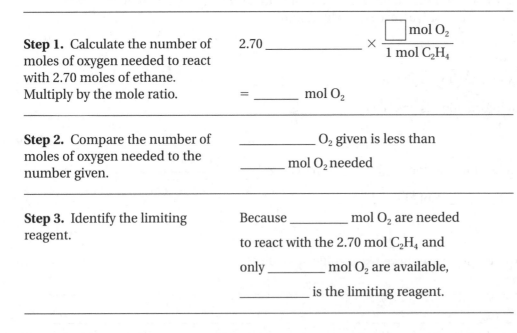

Step 1. Calculate the number of moles of oxygen needed to react with 2.70 moles of ethane. Multiply by the mole ratio.

$$2.70 \text{_____} \times \frac{\boxed{} \text{ mol } O_2}{1 \text{ mol } C_2H_4}$$

$$= \text{_____ mol } O_2$$

Step 2. Compare the number of moles of oxygen needed to the number given.

_____ O_2 given is less than

_____ mol O_2 needed

Step 3. Identify the limiting reagent.

Because _____ mol O_2 are needed

to react with the 2.70 mol C_2H_4 and

only _____ mol O_2 are available,

_____ is the limiting reagent.

b. Calculate the number of moles of water produced.

Step 1. Identify the mole ratio needed.	$\dfrac{\boxed{}\ \text{mol}\ H_2O}{3\ \text{mol}\ O_2}$

Step 2. Calculate the given number of moles of oxygen.	$6.30\ \underline{\hspace{1cm}} \times \dfrac{\boxed{}\ \text{mol}\ H_2O}{3\ \text{mol}\ O_2}$ $= \underline{\hspace{1cm}}\ \text{mol}\ H_2O$

GUIDED PRACTICE PROBLEM 27 (page 258)

27. When 84.8 grams of iron(III) oxide reacts with an excess of carbon monoxide, 54.3 grams of iron are produced.

$$Fe_2O_3(s)\ +\ 3CO(g) \longrightarrow 2Fe(s)\ +\ 3CO_2(g)$$

What is the percent yield of this reaction?

Step 1. First calculate the theoretical yield. Begin by finding the molar mass of Fe_2O_3.	$2\ \text{mol}\ Fe \times (\underline{\hspace{1cm}}\ \text{g}\ Fe/\text{mol}\ Fe)\ +$ $3\ \text{mol}\ O_3 \times (\underline{\hspace{1cm}}\ \text{g}\ O_3/\text{mol}\ O_3)$ $= \underline{\hspace{1cm}}\ \text{g}\ +\ 48.0\ \text{g}$ $= \underline{\hspace{1cm}}\ \text{g}$

Step 2. Calculate the number of moles of iron(III) oxide. Multiply by the mole/mass conversion factor.	$\underline{\hspace{1cm}}\ \text{g}\ Fe_2O_3 \times \dfrac{1\ \text{mol}\ Fe_2O_3}{159.6\ \text{g}\ Fe_2O_3}$ $= \underline{\hspace{1cm}}\ \text{mol}$

Step 3. Find the number of moles of Fe expected. Multiply by the mole ratio.	$0.531\ \underline{\hspace{1cm}} \times \dfrac{\boxed{}\ \text{mol}\ Fe}{1\ \text{mol}\ Fe_2O_3}$ $= \underline{\hspace{1cm}}\ \text{mol}\ Fe$

Step 4. Find the mass of iron that should be produced. Multiply by the mole/mass conversion factor.	$1.062\ \underline{\hspace{1cm}} \times \dfrac{\boxed{}\ \text{g}\ Fe}{1\ \text{mol}\ Fe} = 59.3\ \text{g}\ Fe$

Step 5. Compare the actual yield to the theoretical yield by dividing.	$\dfrac{\text{actual yield}}{\text{theoretical yield}} = \dfrac{\boxed{}\ \text{g}\ Fe}{\boxed{}\ \text{g}\ Fe} = 0.916$

Step 6. Write the answer as a percent, with the correct number of significant figures.	$0.916 = \underline{\hspace{2cm}}$

10 STATES OF MATTER

SECTION 10.1 THE NATURE OF GASES (pages 267–272)

This section describes how the kinetic theory applies to gases. It defines gas pressure and explains how temperature is related to the kinetic energy of the particles of a substance.

▶ Kinetic Theory (page 267)

Match the correct state of matter with each description of water by writing a letter on each line.

_____ 1. tap water   **a.** solid

_____ 2. steam   **b.** liquid

_____ 3. ice   **c.** gas

4. A substance may change from one state to another after a change in

_____ .

5. The energy an object has because of its motion is called

_____ .

6. Circle the letter of each sentence that is true about the assumptions of the kinetic theory concerning gases.

   a. A gas is composed of particles with insignificant volume that are relatively far apart from each other.

   b. Strong attractive forces exist between particles of a gas.

   c. Gases tend to collect near the bottom of a container.

   d. The paths of uninterrupted travel of gas particles are relatively short because the particles are constantly colliding with each other or with other objects.

7. Is the following statement true or false? According to the kinetic theory, collisions between gas particles are perfectly elastic because kinetic energy is transferred without loss from one particle to another, and the total kinetic energy remains constant. _____

▶ Gas Pressure (pages 268–269)

8. Simultaneous collisions of billions of gas particles with an object

   result in _____ .

© Prentice-Hall, Inc.

CHAPTER 10, States of Matter *(continued)*

9. Gas pressure is defined as the force exerted by a gas per _____

_____ .

10. What force holds air molecules in Earth's atmosphere? _____

11. Circle the letter next to every name of a unit of pressure.

    a. mm Hg   **d.** kPa

    b. standard   **e.** atm

    c. pascal   **f.** degree

12. What kind of pressure is measured with a barometer?

_____

13. Look at Figure 10.2 on page 269. What accounts for the difference in heights of the two mercury columns shown in the figure?

_____

_____

_____

_____

14. Standard temperature and pressure (STP) are defined as _____

_____

▶ Kinetic Energy and Kelvin Temperature (pages 269–272)

15. What happens when heat is transferred to a substance so that the average kinetic energy of its particles increases?

_____

16. Circle the letter of the scale that correctly completes this sentence. Temperature on the _____ scale is directly proportional to the average kinetic energy of the particles of a substance.

    a. Celsius

    b. Kelvin

    c. Fahrenheit

    d. Centigrade

17. On the graph below, write the labels *lower temperature* and *higher temperature* to identify the curve that depicts the kinetic energy distribution of particles in a liquid at a lower temperature and at a higher temperature.

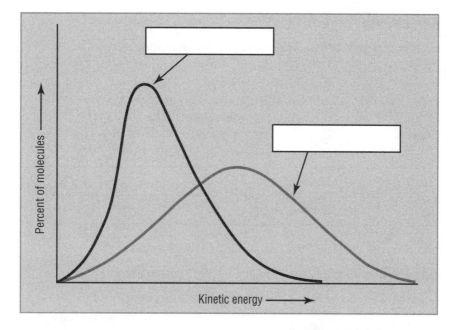

SECTION 10.2 THE NATURE OF LIQUIDS (pages 274–279)

This section describes a model for liquids in terms of the attractive forces between the liquid particles. It also uses kinetic theory to distinguish between evaporation and boiling.

▶ A Model for Liquids (page 274)

1. Is the following sentence true or false? The kinetic theory states that, like particles of a gas, there is no force of attraction between particles of a liquid.

_____

2. Circle the letter next to each sentence that is true about the particles of a liquid.

   a. There is no contribution to kinetic energy from the vibrating or spinning motions of liquid particles.

   b. Most of the particles of a substance in a liquid state have enough kinetic energy to escape into a gaseous state.

   c. Liquids are much denser than gases because intermolecular forces reduce the amount of space between the particles in a liquid.

   d. Increasing pressure on a liquid has hardly any effect on its volume.

   e. Liquid particles are free to slide past one another.

CHAPTER 10, States of Matter *(continued)*

▶ Evaporation (pages 275–277)

3. The conversion of a liquid to a gas or vapor is called _____ .

4. When vaporization occurs at the surface of a liquid that is not boiling, the

process is called _____ .

5. As a liquid evaporates, why do only some of the molecules break away from the surface of the liquid? Why does the liquid evaporate faster if the temperature is increased?

_____

_____

_____

6. Is the following sentence true or false? Evaporation is a cooling process

because particles in a liquid with the highest kinetic energy tend to escape

first, leaving the remaining particles with a lower average kinetic energy and,

thus, a lower temperature. _____

Questions 7, 8, 9, and 10 refer to either container A or container B below. Think of each container as a system involving both liquid water and water vapor.

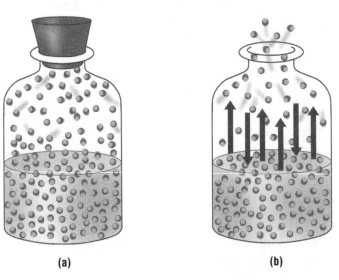

(a)   (b)

7. From which of the containers are water molecules able to escape? ____

8. In which container can a dynamic equilibrium between water molecules in

the liquid state and water molecules in the vapor state be established? ____

9. In which container will the water level remain constant? ____

10. From which container is it possible for all of the liquid water to disappear

through evaporation? ____

11. What causes the chill you may feel after stepping out of a swimming pool on a warm, windy day?

_____

_____

12. Circle the letter next to each sentence that is true about vapor pressure.

   a. Vapor pressure arises when particles of a liquid in a closed, partly filled container vaporize and collide with the walls of the container.

   b. After a time in a closed, partly filled container, a liquid will evaporate and its vapor will condense at equal rates.

   c. Look at Figure 10.8 on page 276. Condensation on the inside of the terrarium indicates that there is not a liquid-vapor equilibrium in the sealed terrarium.

   d. When the temperature of a contained liquid increases, its vapor pressure increases.

13. Look at Figure 10.9 on page 277. How does the vapor pressure of the ethanol in the manometer change when the temperature is increased from 0 °C to 20 °C? Circle the letter of the correct answer.

   a. The vapor pressure decreases by over 4 kPa.

   b. The vapor pressure remains constant.

   c. The vapor pressure increases by over 4 kPa.

   d. There is no way to detect a change in vapor pressure with a manometer.

▶ **Boiling Point** (pages 277–279)

14. The boiling point of a liquid is the temperature at which the vapor pressure of the liquid is just equal to the _____ .

15. Look at Figure 10.10 on page 278. Why does the boiling point temperature decrease as altitude increases?

_____

_____

_____

16. Use Figure 10.11 on page 279. At approximately what temperature would ethanol boil atop Mount Everest, where the atmospheric pressure is 34 kPa? Circle the letter next to the best estimate.

   a. 50 °C   b. 100 °C   c. 0 °C   d. 85 °C

17. Is the following sentence true or false? After a liquid reaches its boiling point, its temperature continues to rise until all the liquid vaporizes. _____

CHAPTER 10, States of Matter *(continued)*

📖 Reading Skill Practice

Writing a summary can help you remember what you have read. When you write a summary, include only the most important points. Write a summary about the boiling point of liquids from pages 277–279. Do your work on a separate sheet of paper.

SECTION 10.3 THE NATURE OF SOLIDS (pages 280–283)

This section describes the highly organized structures of solids, distinguishes between a crystal lattice and a unit cell, and explains how allotropes of an element differ.

▶ A Model for Solids (page 280)

1. Is the following sentence true or false? Although particles in liquids have kinetic energy, the motion of particles in solids is restricted to small vibrations about fixed points. _____

2. Circle the letter next to each sentence that is true about the structure of solids.

   a. A solid melts when the organization of its particles breaks down.

   b. During freezing, particles that form a solid lose kinetic energy so that attractive interactions are able to hold them near fixed positions.

   c. In ionic solids, where the forces holding particles together are relatively stronger, melting points are generally lower than in other solids.

3. Is the following sentence true or false? The temperature at which the liquid and solid states of a substance are in equilibrium is the same as the melting point *and* the freezing point of the substance. _____

4. What type of solid has a relatively low melting point?

   _____

5. Do all solids melt when heated? Explain.

   _____

▶ Crystal Structure and Unit Cells (pages 280–283)

6. How are particles arranged in a crystal lattice?

   _____

© Prentice-Hall, Inc.

7. Circle the letter next to each sentence that is true about crystalline solids.

    a. Most solid substances are not crystalline.

    b. All crystals have sides, or faces, that intersect at angles that are characteristic for a given substance.

    c. There are seven groups, or crystal systems, into which all crystals may be classified.

    d. The regular array of sodium ions and chloride ions gives crystals of table salt their regular shape.

Identify the unit cell in each figure below as simple cubic, body-centered cubic, or face-centered cubic.

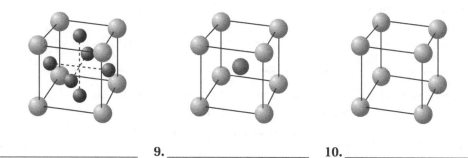

8. _____   **9.** _____   **10.** _____

11. Is the following sentence true or false? Some solid substances can exist in more than one form. Give an example to support your answer.

_____

_____

12. Two or more different molecular forms of the same element in the same physical state are called _____ .

13. What is an amorphous solid?

_____

14. Circle the letter next to each solid that is an amorphous solid.

    a. table salt   **c.** plastic

    b. rubber   **d.** glass

15. How are glasses different from crystalline solids?

_____

_____

_____

CHAPTER 10, States of Matter *(continued)*

SECTION 10.4 CHANGES OF STATE (pages 284–286)

This section explains phase changes between solid, liquid, and vapor states and how to interpret a phase diagram. It also describes the process of sublimation.

▶ **Phase Diagrams** (pages 284–285)

1. What does a phase diagram show?

   _____

   _____

2. What is the triple point of a substance?

   _____

   _____

3. In the phase diagram for water shown below, label the melting point and boiling point at normal atmospheric pressure, and the triple point.

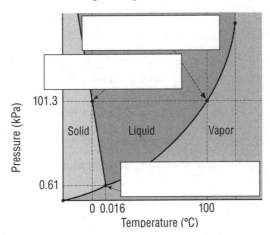

4. Use the phase diagram above to answer the following question. Why is a laboratory required to produce the conditions necessary for observing water at the triple point?

   _____

   _____

▶ **Sublimation** (pages 285–286)

5. The process by which wet laundry dries on an outdoor clothesline in winter

   is called _____ .

6. Is the following sentence true or false? Solids have vapor pressure because some particles near the surface of a solid substance have enough kinetic energy to escape directly into the vapor phase. _____

MathWise

GUIDED PRACTICE PROBLEM 2 (page 271)

2. The pressure at the top of Mount Everest is 33.7 kPa. Is that pressure greater than or less than 0.25 atm?

Analyze

Step 1. To convert kPa to atm, what conversion factor do you need to use?

_____

Step 2. Why can you use an estimate to solve this problem?

_____

_____

Solve

Step 3. Write the expression needed to find the answer.

_____

Step 4. Which common fraction is this number close to?

_____

Step 5. What is this fraction written as a decimal? Is this number greater than or less than 0.25?

_____

Evaluate

Step 6. Are you confident your estimate gave a correct answer to this problem?

_____

_____

EXTRA PRACTICE (similar to Practice Problem 1, page 271)

1. What pressure, in atmospheres, does a gas exert at 152 mm Hg?

What is this pressure in kilopascals?

THERMOCHEMISTRY—HEAT AND CHEMICAL CHANGE

SECTION 11.1 THE FLOW OF ENERGY—HEAT (pages 293–299)

This section explains the relationship between energy and heat, and distinguishes between heat capacity and specific heat.

▶ Energy Transformations (pages 293–294)

1. What area of study in chemistry is concerned with the heat changes that occur during chemical reactions? _____

2. Where the use of energy is concerned (in a scientific sense), when is work done?

_____

3. Circle the letter next to each sentence that is true about energy.

   a. Energy is the capacity for doing work or supplying heat.

   b. Energy is detected only because of its effects.

   c. Heat is energy that transfers from one object to another because they are at the same temperature.

   d. Gasoline contains a significant amount of chemical potential energy.

4. Circle the letter next to each sentence that is true about heat.

   a. One effect of adding heat to a substance is an increase in the temperature of that substance.

   b. Heat always flows from a cooler object to a warmer object.

   c. If two objects remain in contact, heat will flow from the warmer object to the cooler object until the temperature of both objects is the same.

▶ Exothermic and Endothermic Processes (pages 294–295)

5. What can be considered the "system" and what are the "surroundings" when studying a mixture of chemicals undergoing a reaction? Write your answers where indicated below.

System: _____

_____

Surroundings: _____

_____

CHAPTER 11, Thermochemistry—Heat and Chemical Change *(continued)*

6. In thermochemical calculations, is the direction of heat flow given from the point of view of the system, or of the surroundings?

_____

7. What universal law states that energy can neither be created nor destroyed and can always be accounted for as work, stored potential energy, or heat?

_____

Questions 8 through 12 refer to the systems and surroundings illustrated in diagrams (a) and (b) below.

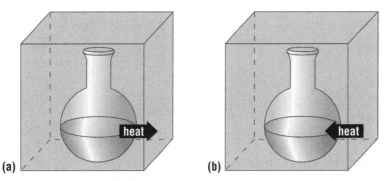

8. Which diagram illustrates an endothermic process? _____

9. Is heat flow positive or negative in diagram (a)? _____

10. Which diagram illustrates an exothermic process? _____

11. Is heat flow positive or negative in diagram (b)? _____

12. What does a negative value for heat represent?

_____

To answer Questions 13 and 14, look at Figure 11.4 on page 295.

13. A system is a person sitting next to a campfire. Is this system endothermic or exothermic? Explain why.

_____

_____

14. A system is a person who is perspiring. Is this system endothermic or exothermic? Explain why.

_____

_____

_____

▶ **Heat Capacity and Specific Heat** (pages 295–297)

15. Heat generated by the human body is usually measured in units called

    _____ .

16. Describe the chemical reaction that generates heat in the human body.

    _____

17. What is the definition of a calorie?

    _____

    _____

18. How is the calorie (written with a lower case c) related to the dietary Calorie (written with a capital C)?

    _____

19. Circle the letter next to the SI unit of heat and energy.

    a. calorie

    b. Calorie

    c. joule

    d. Celsius degree

20. Is the next sentence true or false? Samples of two different substances having

    the same mass always have the same heat capacity. _____

21. Compare the heat capacity of a 2-kg steel frying pan and a 2-g steel pin. If the heat capacities of these objects differ, explain why.

    _____

22. Is the next sentence true or false? The specific heat of a substance varies with

    the mass of the sample. _____

SECTION 11.2 MEASURING AND EXPRESSING HEAT CHANGES (pages 300–306)

This section explains how to construct equations and perform calculations that show heat changes for chemical and physical processes.

▶ **Calorimetry** (pages 300–303)

1. The property that is useful for keeping track of heat changes in chemical

   and physical processes at constant pressure is called _____ .

2. What is calorimetry? _____

   _____

CHAPTER 11, Thermochemistry—Heat and Chemical Change *(continued)*

3. Use Figure 11.8 on page 300. Circle the letter next to each sentence that is true about calorimeters.

   a. The calorimeter container is insulated to minimize loss of heat to or absorption of heat from the surroundings.

   b. Because foam cups are excellent heat insulators, they may be used as simple calorimeters.

   c. A stirrer is used to keep temperatures uneven in a calorimeter.

   d. In the calorimeter shown in Figure 11.8, the chemical substances dissolved in water constitute the system and the water is part of the surroundings.

4. Is the following sentence true or false? For systems at constant pressure, heat change and enthalpy change are the same thing. _____

5. Complete the table below to show the direction of heat flow and type of reaction for positive and negative change of enthalpy.

Sign of Enthalpy Change	Direction of Heat Flow	Is Reaction Endothermic or Exothermic?
ΔH is positive ($\Delta H > 0$)		
ΔH is negative ($\Delta H < 0$)		

6. Name each quantity that is represented in the equation for heat change in an aqueous solution.

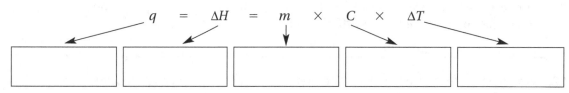

$$q \quad = \quad \Delta H \quad = \quad m \quad \times \quad C \quad \times \quad \Delta T$$

▶ Thermochemical Equations *(pages 303–306)*

7. What happens to the temperature of water after calcium oxide is added?

   _____

8. A chemical equation that includes the heat change is called a _____ equation.

9. Why is it important to give the physical state of the reactants and products in a thermochemical equation?

   _____

   _____

10. Complete the enthalpy diagram for the combustion of natural gas. Use the thermochemical equation in the first paragraph on page 306 as a guide.

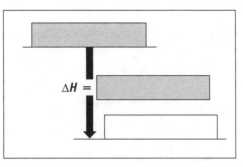

$\Delta H =$

SECTION 11.3 HEAT IN CHANGES OF STATE (pages 307–313)

This section explains heat changes that occur during melting, freezing, boiling, and condensing.

▶ Heats of Fusion and Solidification (pages 307–309)

1. Is the following sentence true or false? A piece of ice placed in a bowl in a warm room will remain at a temperature of 0 °C until all of the ice has melted.

_____

2. Circle the letter next to each sentence that is true about heat of fusion and heat of solidification of a given substance.

   a. The molar heat of fusion is the negative of the molar heat of solidification.

   b. Heat is released during melting and absorbed during freezing.

   c. Heat is absorbed during melting and released during freezing.

   d. The quantity of heat absorbed during melting is exactly the same as the quantity of heat released when the liquid solidifies.

3. Use Table 11.5 on page 308. Determine ΔH for each of these physical changes.

   a. $H_2(s) \longrightarrow H_2(l)$ $\Delta H =$ _____

   b. $Ne(s) \longrightarrow Ne(l)$ $\Delta H =$ _____

   c. $O_2(s) \longrightarrow O_2(l)$ $\Delta H =$ _____

▶ Heats of Vaporization and Condensation (pages 310–311)

4. Is the following sentence true or false? As liquids absorb heat at their boiling points, the temperature remains constant while they vaporize.

_____

CHAPTER 11, Thermochemistry—Heat and Chemical Change (*continued*)

Use the heating curve for water shown below to answer Questions 5, 6, and 7.

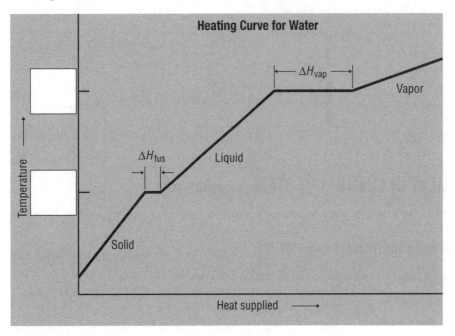

5. Label the melting point and boiling point temperatures on the graph.

6. What happens to the temperature during melting and vaporization?

_____

_____

7. Circle the letter next to the process that *releases* the most heat.

   a. Melting of 1 mol of water at 0 °C

   b. Freezing of 1 mol of water at 0 °C

   c. Vaporization of 1 mol of water at 100 °C

   d. Condensation of 1 mol of water at 100 °C

Look at Table 11.5 on page 308 to help you answer Questions 8, 9, and 10.

8. How many of the 13 substances listed have a higher molar heat of vaporization

   than water? Which one(s)? _____

9. Which two of the thirteen substances listed have a freezing point within 20 °C

   of room temperature? _____

10. Which substance listed has a freezing point and a boiling point that are

    nearest to absolute zero? _____

▶ Heat of Solution (pages 312–313)

11. The heat change caused by dissolution of one mole of a substance is the

_____ .

12. How does a cold pack containing water and ammonium nitrate work?

_____

_____

_____

Reading Skill Practice

Writing a summary can help you remember the information you have read. When you write a summary, write only the most important points. Write a summary for each of the five types of heat changes described on pages 307–313. Your summary should be much shorter than these six pages of text. Do your work on another sheet of paper.

SECTION 11.4 CALCULATING HEAT CHANGES (pages 314–318)

This section explains how Hess's law of heat summation and standard heats of formation may be applied to find heat changes for a series of chemical and physical processes.

▶ Hess's Law (pages 314–316)

1. For reactions that occur in a series of steps, Hess's law of heat summation says that if you add the thermochemical equations for each step to give a final equation for the reaction, you may also _____

_____ .

2. Is the following sentence true or false? Graphite is a more stable form of elemental carbon than diamond at 25 °C, so diamond will slowly change to graphite over an extremely long period of time. _____

3. Look at Figures 11.17 and 11.18 on page 315. According to Hess's Law, the enthalpy change from diamond to carbon dioxide can be expressed as the sum of what three enthalpy changes?

   a. _____

   b. _____

   c. _____

CHAPTER 11, Thermochemistry—Heat and Chemical Change *(continued)*

▶ Standard Heats of Formation (pages 316–318)

4. The change in enthalpy that accompanies the formation of one mole of a compound from its elements with all substances in their standard states at 25 °C and 101.3 kPa is called the _____ .

5. Is the following sentence true or false? Chemists have set the standard heat of formation of free elements, including elements that occur in nature as diatomic molecules, at zero. _____

6. Complete the enthalpy diagram below by finding the heat of formation when hydrogen and chlorine gases combine to form hydrogen chloride at 25 °C. Use the data in Table 11.6 on page 316 and the equation $\Delta H^0 = \Delta H_f^0$ (products) − ΔH_f^0 (reactants) to find the answer.

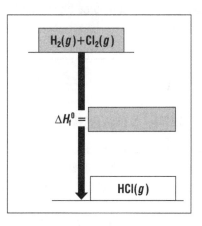

7. Look at Table 11.6. Methane burns to form carbon dioxide and water vapor.

$$CH_4(g) + 2O_2(g) \longrightarrow CO_2(g) + 2H_2O(g)$$

a. Will the heat of this reaction be positive or negative? How do you know?

_____

_____

_____

b. How does your experience confirm that your answer to Question 7a is reasonable?

_____

_____

© Prentice-Hall, Inc.

MathWise

GUIDED PRACTICE PROBLEM 1 (page 299)

1. When 435 J of heat is added to 3.4 g of olive oil at 21 °C, the temperature increases to 85 °C. What is the specific heat of olive oil?

Analyze

a. What is the formula for calculating specific heat? _____

b. What are the knowns and the unknown in this problem?

Knowns: Unknown:

m = _____   _____

q = _____

ΔT = _____

Solve

c. Substitute the known values into the equation for specific heat and solve.

$$C_{\text{olive oil}} = \boxed{} = 2.0 \boxed{}$$

Evaluate

d. Explain why you think your answer is reasonable. Think about the time it takes to fry foods in olive oil versus the time it takes to cook foods in boiling water.

_____

_____

_____

_____

_____

e. Are the units in your answer correct? How do you know?

_____

_____

CHAPTER 11, Thermochemistry—Heat and Chemical Change *(continued)*

GUIDED PRACTICE PROBLEM 11 (page 302)

11. A student mixed 50.0 mL of water containing 0.50 mol HCl at 22.5 °C with 50.0 mL of water containing 0.50 mol NaOH at 22.5 °C in a foam cup calorimeter. The temperature of the resulting solution increased to 26.0 °C. How much heat in kilojoules (kJ) was released by this reaction?

   a. Calculate the final volume of the water. V_{final} = 50.0 mL + 50.0 mL = _____

   b. Calculate the total mass of the water, using the density of water. m = _____ mL × $\dfrac{\boxed{}\ \text{g}}{\text{mL}}$ = _____

   c. Calculate ΔT. ΔT = 26.0 °C − _____ °C = _____ °C

   d. Substitute the known quantities into the equation for changes in enthalpy (ΔH). ΔH = (_____ g) × (4.18 _____) × _____ °C

   e. Solve. _____ J

   f. Convert joules to kilojoules (kJ) and round to three significant figures. _____ J × $\dfrac{1\ \text{kJ}}{1000\ \text{J}}$ = _____ kJ

EXTRA PRACTICE (similar to Practice Problem 13, page 304)

13. When carbon disulfide is formed from its elements, heat is absorbed. Calculate the amount of heat (in kJ) absorbed when 8.53 g of carbon disulfide is formed.

   $$C(s) + 2S(s) \longrightarrow CS_2(l) \qquad\qquad \Delta H = 89.3\ \text{kJ}$$

GUIDED PRACTICE PROBLEM 20 (page 309)

20. How many grams of ice at 0 °C and 101.3 kPa could be melted by the addition of 0.400 kJ of heat? Find the molar heat of fusion in Table 11.5.

   a. Write the conversion factors from ΔH_{fus} and the molar mass of ice. $\dfrac{1\ \text{mol ice}}{\boxed{}\ \text{kJ}}$ and $\dfrac{\boxed{}\ \text{g ice}}{1\ \text{mol ice}}$

   b. Multiply the known heat change by the conversion factors.

EXTRA PRACTICE (similar to Practice Problem 22, page 311)

22. How much heat (in kJ) is absorbed when 88.45 g $H_2O(l)$ at 100 °C is converted to steam at 100 °C? Find the molar heat of vaporization in Table 11.5.

12 THE BEHAVIOR OF GASES

SECTION 12.1 THE PROPERTIES OF GASES (pages 327–328)

This section describes the properties of gas particles and explains how the kinetic energy of gas particles relates to Kelvin temperature.

▶ Kinetic Theory Revisited (pages 327–328)

1. What theory explains the behavior of gases with respect to conditions such as temperature and pressure? _____

2. If you notice that a sealed bag of potato chips bulges when placed near a sunny window, what can you hypothesize about the relationship between the temperature and pressure of an enclosed gas?

   _____

3. List three basic assumptions of the kinetic theory about the properties of gases.

   a. _____

   _____

   b. _____

   _____

   c. _____

   _____

4. Circle the letter next to each sentence that is true concerning the compressibility of gases.

   a. The large relative distances between gas particles means that there is considerable empty space between them.

   b. The assumption that gas particles are far apart explains gas compressibility.

   c. Compressibility is a measure of how much the volume of matter decreases under pressure.

   d. Energy is released by a gas when it is compressed.

5. Look at Figure 12.1 on page 327. How does an automobile air bag protect the crash dummy from being broken as a result of impact?

   _____

   _____

CHAPTER 12, The Behavior of Gases *(continued)*

▶ **Variables That Describe a Gas** *(page 328)*

6. List the name, the symbol, and a common unit for the four variables that are generally used to describe the characteristics of a gas.

   a. _____

   b. _____

   c. _____

   d. _____

7. List four everyday items that rely on the behavior of gases to operate properly.

   _____

   _____

   _____

SECTION 12.2 FACTORS AFFECTING GAS PRESSURE *(pages 330–332)*

This section explains how gas pressure is affected by the amount of gas, the volume of a container, and temperature changes.

▶ **Amount of Gas** *(pages 330–331)*

1. How do conditions change inside a tire when you pump it up with a tire

   pump? _____

2. The diagrams below show a sealed container at three pressures. Complete the labels showing the gas pressure in each container.

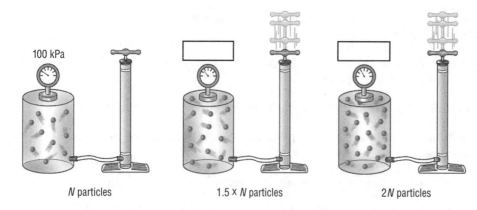

   N particles   1.5 × N particles   2N particles

3. What can happen if too much air is pumped into a tire?

   _____

   _____

4. Is the following sentence true or false? When a sealed container of gas is opened, gas will flow from the region of lower pressure to the region of higher pressure. _____

5. Look at Figure 12.7 on page 331. What happens when the spray button on an aerosol spray can is pressed?

_____

_____

_____

▶ Volume (page 331)

6. In the diagram, complete the labels showing the pressure on the piston and the gas pressure inside the container.

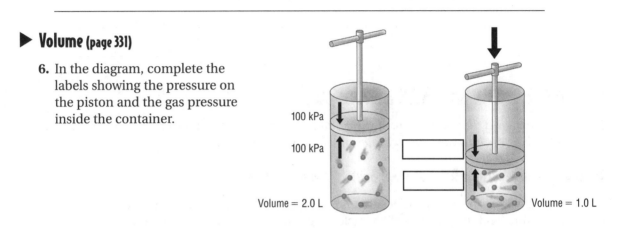

100 kPa

100 kPa

Volume = 2.0 L

Volume = 1.0 L

7. When the volume is reduced by one half, what happens to the pressure?

_____

▶ Temperature (page 332)

8. Is the following sentence true or false? Raising the temperature of an enclosed gas causes its pressure to decrease. _____

9. Circle the letter next to each sentence that correctly describes how gases behave when the temperature increases .

a. The average kinetic energy of the gas particles increases as the particles absorb thermal energy.

b. Faster-moving particles impact the walls of their container with more energy, exerting greater pressure.

c. When the average kinetic energy of enclosed gas particles doubles, temperature doubles and pressure is cut in half.

10. Explain why it is dangerous to throw aerosol cans into a fire.

_____

_____

CHAPTER 12, The Behavior of Gases (continued)

11. How are the average kinetic energy of gas particles and their Kelvin temperature related?

_____

_____

12. Decide whether the following sentence is true or false, and explain your reasoning. When the temperature of a sample of steam increases from 100 °C to 200 °C, the average kinetic energy of its particles doubles.

_____

_____

SECTION 12.3 THE GAS LAWS (pages 333–340)

This section explains the relationship of the volume, pressure, and temperature of gases as described by Boyle's law, Charles's law, Gay-Lussac's law, and the combined gas law.

▶ The Pressure-Volume Relationship: Boyle's Law (page 333–335)

1. Circle the letter of each sentence that is true about the relationship between the volume and the pressure of an enclosed gas held at constant temperature.

   a. When the pressure increases, the volume decreases.

   b. When the pressure decreases, the volume increases.

   c. When the pressure increases, the volume increases.

   d. When the pressure decreases, the volume decreases.

2. What is an inverse relationship for two variables?

_____

3. _____ law states that for a given mass of gas at a constant temperature, the volume of the gas varies inversely with pressure.

Questions 4, 5, 6, and 7 refer to the graph. This graph represents the relationship between pressure and volume for a sample of gas in a container at a constant temperature.

4. $P_1 \times V_1 =$ _____

5. $P_2 \times V_2 =$ _____

6. $P_3 \times V_3 =$ _____

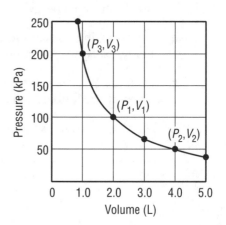

7. What do you notice about the product of pressure times volume at constant temperature? What gas law does this illustrate?

_____

▶ The Temperature-Volume Relationship: Charles's Law (pages 335–337)

8. Look at the graph in Figure 12.11 on page 335. What two observations did Jacques Charles make about the behavior of gases from similar data?

_____

_____

9. The temperature at which average kinetic energy of gas particles theoretically is zero is called _____ .

10. What does it mean to say that two variables are directly proportional?

_____

_____

11. Is the following sentence true or false? Charles's law states that when the pressure of a fixed mass of gas is held constant, the volume of the gas is directly proportional to its Kelvin temperature. _____

12. Charles's law may be written $\dfrac{V_1}{T_1} = \dfrac{V_2}{T_2}$ at constant pressure if the temperatures are measured on what scale? _____

▶ The Temperature-Pressure Relationship: Gay-Lussac's Law (pages 338–339)

13. Complete the following sentence. Gay-Lussac's law states that the pressure of a gas is _____ .

14. Gay-Lussac's law may be written $\dfrac{P_1}{T_1} = \dfrac{P_2}{T_2}$ if the volume is constant and if the temperatures are measured on what scale? _____

15. Complete the missing labels in the diagram below showing the pressure change when a gas is heated at constant volume.

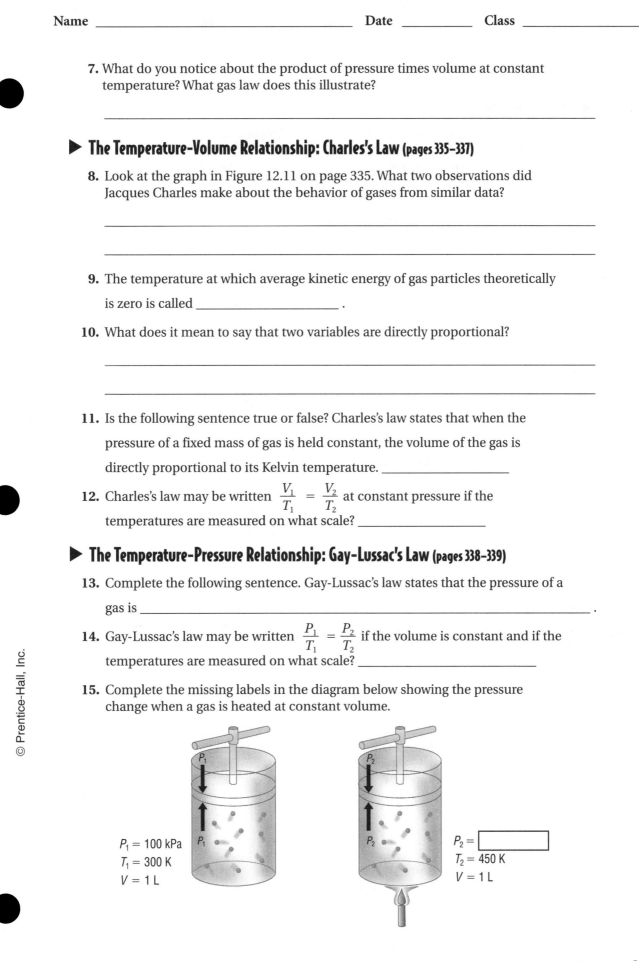

$P_1 = 100$ kPa
$T_1 = 300$ K
$V = 1$ L

$P_2 = $ ☐
$T_2 = 450$ K
$V = 1$ L

CHAPTER 12, The Behavior of Gases *(continued)*

▶ The Combined Gas Law (pages 339–340)

16. Is the following sentence true or false? A single mathematical expression involving pressure, temperature, and volume can represent the gas laws of Boyle, Charles, and Gay-Lussac if one or another of these quantities is held constant.

_____

Questions 17, 18, 19, and 20 refer to the mathematical equation

$$\frac{P_1 \times V_1}{T_1} = \frac{P_2 \times V_2}{T_2}$$

17. What is this mathematical equation called? _____

18. Which gas law does this equation represent if temperature is held constant so that $T_1 = T_2$? _____

19. Which gas law does this equation represent if pressure is held constant so that $P_1 = P_2$? _____

20. Which gas law does this equation represent if volume is held constant so that $V_1 = V_2$? _____

21. In which situations does the combined gas law enable you to do calculations when the other gas laws do not apply?

_____

_____

SECTION 12.4 IDEAL GASES (pages 341–346)

This section explains how to use the ideal gas law to calculate the amount of gas at specified conditions of temperature, pressure and volume. This section also distinguishes between real and ideal gases.

▶ Ideal Gas Law (pages 341–343)

1. In addition to pressure, temperature, and volume, what fourth variable must be considered when analyzing the behavior of a gas in a system?

_____

2. Look at Figure 12.16 on page 341. Assume that pressure, temperature, and volume inside the container are known. What general gas law can be used to calculate the number of moles of gas inside the container?

_____

3. Is the number of moles in a sample of gas directly proportional or inversely proportional to the number of particles of gas in the sample?

_____

© Prentice-Hall, Inc.

4. At a specified temperature and pressure, is the number of moles of gas in a sample directly proportional or inversely proportional to the volume of the sample? _____

5. Circle the letter next to the correct description of how the combined gas law must be modified when you measure the amount of a gas in moles.

   a. Multiply each side of the equation by the number of moles.

   b. Add the number of moles to each side of the equation.

   c. Divide each side of the equation by the number of moles.

6. Which variable in the equation

$$\frac{(P_1 \times V_1)}{(T_1 \times n_1)} = \frac{(P_2 \times V_2)}{(T_2 \times n_2)}$$

is constant in Boyle's law, Charles's law, and Gay-Lussac's law?

_____

7. For what kind of gas is $(P \times V) / (T \times n)$ a constant for all values of pressure, temperature, and volume under which the gas can exist?_____

8. When you know the volume occupied by one mole of gas at standard temperature and pressure, what constant may be evaluated?

_____

9. Complete the table about the ideal gas law. Write what each symbol in the ideal gas law represents, the unit in which it is measured and abbreviation.

Symbol	Quantity	Unit	Abbreviation for Unit
P			
V			
n			
R			
T			

10. Why would you use the ideal gas law when you know the gas constant instead of the combined gas law?

_____

_____

CHAPTER 12, The Behavior of Gases *(continued)*

▶ The Ideal Gas Law and Kinetic Theory (page 344)

11. To meet the assumptions of _____ of gases, gases must behave in an "ideal" way.

12. Circle the letter of each sentence that is true about ideal gases and the kinetic theory.

    a. An ideal gas would not follow the gas laws at all temperatures and pressures.

    b. An ideal gas would not conform to the assumptions of the kinetic theory.

    c. There is no real gas that exactly conforms to the kinetic theory and the ideal gas law.

    d. At many conditions of temperature and pressure, real gases behave very much like ideal gases.

13. Is the following sentence true or false? If a gas were truly an ideal gas, it would be impossible to liquefy or solidify it by cooling or by applying pressure.

_____

14. Look at Figure 12.18 on page 344. What material is illustrated? What change of state is occurring? Is this behavior a property of an ideal gas or real gas?

_____

_____

▶ Departures from the Ideal Gas Law (pages 344–346)

15. A gas that follows the gas laws over a certain range of temperature and

pressure is said to exhibit _____ under those conditions.

16. What ratio always equals 1 for an ideal gas?

_____

Look at the graph in Figure 12.19 on page 344 to answer Questions 17, 18, and 19.

17. What is the magnitude of the marked intervals on the pressure axis of the

graph? _____

18. Which of the gases shown deviates the most from ideal at pressures less than

20 000 kPa? _____

19. Which of the gases shown has behavior that is close to ideal ranging from near 0 kPa to almost 40 000 kPa? _____

20. What are two assumptions of simple kinetic theory that are incorrect for real gases?

   a. _____

   b. _____

21. Is the following statement true or false? The presence of intermolecular forces between gas particles tends to increase volume, making the ratio $(P \times V)/(n \times R \times T)$ greater than 1. _____

22. Is the following statement true or false? The nonzero volume of gas particles tends to increase volume, making the ratio $(P \times V)/(n \times R \times T)$ greater than 1. _____

SECTION 12.5 GAS MOLECULES: MIXTURES AND MOVEMENTS (pages 347–353)

This section explains Avogadro's hypothesis, Dalton's law of partial pressures, and Graham's law of effusion.

▶ Avogadro's Hypothesis (pages 347–349)

1. What is Avogadro's hypothesis?

   _____

   _____

2. Look at Figure 12.21 on page 347 to help you answer this question. Why is Avogadro's hypothesis reasonable?

   _____

   _____

   _____

3. How many gas particles occupy a volume of 22.4 L at standard temperature and pressure? _____

▶ Dalton's Law (pages 350–351)

4. Is the following sentence true or false? Gas pressure depends only on the number of gas particles in a given volume and on their average kinetic energy—the type of particle does not matter. _____

5. The contribution of the pressure of each gas in a mixture to the total pressure is called the _____ exerted by that gas.

CHAPTER 12, The Behavior of Gases *(continued)*

6. What is Dalton's law of partial pressures?

_____

_____

7. Container (T) in the figure below contains a mixture of the three different gases in (a), (b), and (c) at the pressures shown. Write in the pressure in container (T).

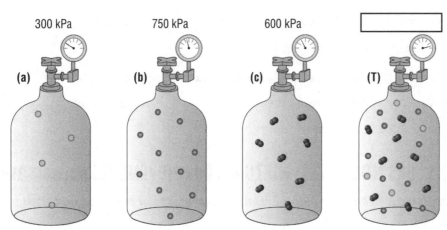

300 kPa   750 kPa   600 kPa

(a)   (b)   (c)   (T)

▶ Graham's Law (pages 352–353)

8. The tendency of gas molecules to move from areas of higher concentration to areas of lower concentration is called _____ .

9. What is Graham's law of effusion?

_____

_____

10. Is the following sentence true or false? If two bodies with different masses have the same kinetic energy, the one with the greater mass must move faster.

_____

📖 Reading Skill Practice

You may sometimes forget the meaning of a key term that was introduced earlier in the textbook. When this happens, you can check its meaning in the Glossary on pages 36–46 of the Reference Section. The Glossary lists all key terms in the textbook and their meanings. You'll find the terms listed in alphabetical order. Use the Glossary to review the meanings of all key terms introduced in Section 12.5. Write each term and its definition on a separate sheet of paper.

© Prentice-Hall, Inc.

MathWise

GUIDED PRACTICE PROBLEM 16 (page 340)

16. A gas at 155 kPa and 25 °C occupies a container with an initial volume of 1.00 L. By changing the volume, the pressure of the gas increases to 605 kPa as the temperature is raised to 125 °C. What is the new volume?

Analyze

a. Temperature can be converted from Celsius to Kelvin by adding _____ .

b. What is the expression for the combined gas law?

_____

c. What is the unknown in this problem? _____

Calculate

d. Convert degrees Celsius to kelvins.

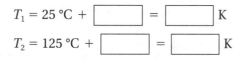

$T_1 = 25\,°C +$ ☐ $=$ ☐ K

$T_2 = 125\,°C +$ ☐ $=$ ☐ K

e. Rearrange the combined gas law to isolate V_2.

$V_2 =$

f. Substitute the known quantities into the equation and solve.

$$V_2 = \frac{1.00\,L \times \boxed{}\ \text{kPa} \times 398\,\text{K}}{605\,\text{kPa} \times \boxed{}\ \text{K}} = \boxed{}$$

Evaluate

g. Explain why you think your answer is reasonable.

_____

_____

_____

_____

h. Are the units in your answer correct? How do you know?

_____

CHAPTER 12, The Behavior of Gases *(continued)*

EXTRA PRACTICE (similar to Practice Problem 14, page 338)

14. A gas has a pressure of 7.50 kPa at 420 K. What will the pressure be at 210 K if the volume does not change?

_____

GUIDED PRACTICE PROBLEM 25 (page 343)

25. What volume will 12.0 g of oxygen gas, $O_2(g)$, occupy at 25 °C and a pressure of 52.7 kPa?

_____

Step 1. Convert grams to moles of O_2.

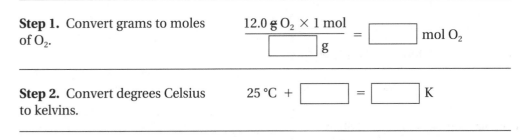

$$\frac{12.0 \text{ g } O_2 \times 1 \text{ mol}}{\boxed{} \text{ g}} = \boxed{} \text{ mol } O_2$$

Step 2. Convert degrees Celsius to kelvins.

$$25\,°C + \boxed{} = \boxed{} \text{ K}$$

Step 3. Substitute the known quantities into the ideal gas law and solve for *V*.

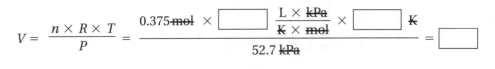

$$V = \frac{n \times R \times T}{P} = \frac{0.375 \cancel{\text{mol}} \times \boxed{} \dfrac{L \times \cancel{kPa}}{\cancel{K} \times \cancel{mol}} \times \boxed{} \cancel{K}}{52.7 \cancel{kPa}} = \boxed{}$$

EXTRA PRACTICE (similar to Practice Problem 23, page 342)

23. What pressure will be exerted by 0.500 mol of a gas at 25 °C if it is contained in a 0.619-L vessel?

GUIDED PRACTICE PROBLEM 33 (page 348)

33. How many nitrogen molecules are in 5.12 L of the gas at STP?

_____

Step 1. Write the conversion factor for volume to moles for a gas at STP.

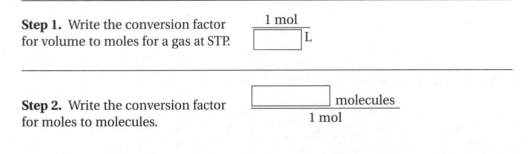

$$\frac{1 \text{ mol}}{\boxed{} \text{ L}}$$

Step 2. Write the conversion factor for moles to molecules.

$$\frac{\boxed{} \text{ molecules}}{1 \text{ mol}}$$

Step 3. Multiply the known value by the conversion factors.

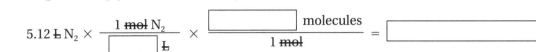

$$5.12 \, \cancel{L} \, N_2 \times \frac{1 \, \cancel{mol} \, N_2}{\boxed{} \, \cancel{L}} \times \frac{\boxed{} \, \text{molecules}}{1 \, \cancel{mol}} = \boxed{}$$

EXTRA PRACTICE (similar to Practice Problem 31, page 348)

31. What is the volume occupied by 0.50 mol of a gas at STP?

EXTRA PRACTICE (similar to Practice Problem 35, page 349)

35. What is the volume of a container that holds 4.40 g of carbon dioxide at STP?

GUIDED PRACTICE PROBLEM 37 (page 351)

37. Determine the total pressure of a gas mixture that contains oxygen, nitrogen, and helium if the partial pressures of the gases are as follows:

$P_{O_2} = 20.0$ kPa, $P_{N_2} = 46.7$ kPa, and $P_{He} = 26.7$ kPa.

Analyze

a. What is the expression for Dalton's law of partial pressure?

_____

b. What is the unknown in this problem? _____

Calculate

c. Substitute the known quantities into the equation and solve.

Evaluate

d. Why is your answer reasonable?

_____

_____

13 ELECTRONS IN ATOMS

SECTION 13.1 MODELS OF THE ATOM (pages 361–366)

This section summarizes the development of atomic theory. It also explains the significance of quantized energies of electrons as they relate to the quantum mechanical model of the atom.

▶ The Evolution of Atomic Models (pages 361–363)

1. What are the chemical properties of atoms, ions, and molecules related to?

   _____

2. Complete the table about atomic models and the scientists who developed them.

Scientist	Model of Atom
Dalton	
Thomson	
Rutherford	
Bohr	

3. The energy level of an electron is the region around the nucleus where

   _____ .

4. Is the following sentence true or false? The electrons in an atom can exist

   between energy levels. _____

5. Circle the letter of the term that completes the sentence correctly. A quantum of energy is the amount of energy required to

   a. move an electron from its present energy level to the next lower one

   b. maintain an electron in its present energy level

   c. move an electron from its present energy level to the next higher one

6. In general, the higher the electron is on the energy ladder, the

   _____ it is from the nucleus.

© Prentice-Hall, Inc.

CHAPTER 13, Electrons in Atoms *(continued)*

▶ The Quantum Mechanical Model *(pages 363–364)*

7. What is the difference between the previous models of the atom and the modern quantum mechanical model? _____

_____

8. Is the following sentence true or false? The quantum mechanical model of the atom estimates the probability of finding an electron in a certain position.

_____

▶ Atomic Orbitals *(pages 364–366)*

9. Circle the letter of the term that correctly answers this question. Which name describes the major energy levels of electrons?

   a. atomic orbitals   **c.** quantas

   b. quantum mechanical numbers   **d.** principal quantum numbers (n)

10. Principal energy levels are assigned values in order of _____ energy: $n = 1, 2, 3, 4$, and so forth.

11. In the quantum mechanical model the regions where electrons are likely

    to be found are called _____ and are denoted by

    _____ .

12. Match each diagram below with the name of its p orbital, the p_x, p_y, or p_z.

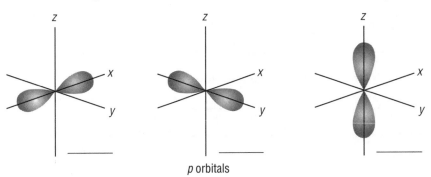

p orbitals

13. Use the diagram above. Describe how the p_x, p_y, and p_z orbitals are similar.

_____

14. Describe how the p_x, p_y, and p_z orbitals are different. _____

_____

15. Circle the letter of the formula for the maximum number of electrons that can occupy a principal energy level. Use n for the principal quantum number.

   a. $2n^2$ **b.** n^2 **c.** $2n$ **d.** n

SECTION 13.2 ELECTRON ARRANGEMENT IN ATOMS (pages 367–370)

This section shows you how to apply the aufbau principle, the Pauli exclusion principle, and Hund's rule to help you write the electron configurations of elements. It also explains why the electron configurations for some elements differ from those assigned using the aufbau principle.

▶ Electron Configurations (pages 367–369)

1. The ways in which electrons are arranged around the nuclei of atoms are

    called _____ .

Match the name of the rule used to find the electron configurations of atoms with the rule itself.

_____ **2.** aufbau principle

_____ **3.** Pauli exclusion principle

_____ **4.** Hund's rule

    a. When electrons occupy orbitals of equal energy, one electron enters each orbital until all the orbitals contain one electron with parallel spins.

    b. Electrons enter orbitals of lowest energy first.

    c. An atomic orbital may describe at most two electrons.

5. Look at the aufbau diagram, Figure 13.6 on page 367. Which atomic orbital

    is of higher energy, a $4f$ or a $5p$ orbital? _____

6. Fill in the electron configurations for the elements given in the table. Use the orbital filling diagrams to complete the table.

Electron Configurations for Some Selected Elements							
	Orbital filling						Electron configuration
Element	1s	2s	2p$_x$	2p$_y$	2p$_z$	3s	
☐	↑	☐	☐	☐	☐	☐	$1s^2$
He	↑↓	☐	☐	☐	☐	☐	
☐	↑↓	↑	☐	☐	☐	☐	$1s^2 2s^1$
C	↑↓	↑↓	↑	↑	☐	☐	
☐	↑↓	↑↓	↑	↑	↑	☐	$1s^2 2s^2 2p^3$
O	↑↓	↑↓	↑↓	↑	↑	☐	
☐	↑↓	↑↓	↑↓	↑↓	↑	☐	$1s^2 2s^2 2p^5$
Ne	↑↓	↑↓	↑↓	↑↓	↑↓	☐	
☐	↑↓	↑↓	↑↓	↑↓	↑↓	↑	$1s^2 2s^2 2p^6 3s^1$

CHAPTER 13, Electrons in Atoms *(continued)*

7. In the shorthand method for writing an electron configuration, what does a superscript stand for?

_____

8. In the shorthand method for writing an electron configuration, what does the sum of the superscripts equal?

_____

▶ Exceptional Electron Configurations (page 370)

9. Is the following sentence true or false? The aufbau principle works for every element in the periodic table. _____

10. Filled energy sublevels are more _____ than partially filled sublevels.

11. Half-filled levels are not as stable as _____ levels, but are more stable than other configurations.

Reading Skill Practice

Outlining can help you understand and remember what you have read. Prepare an outline of Section 13.2, *Electron Arrangement in Atoms.* Begin your outline by copying the headings from the textbook. Under each heading, write the main idea. Then list the details that support, or back up, the main idea. Do your work on a separate sheet of paper.

SECTION 13.3 PHYSICS AND THE QUANTUM MECHANICAL MODEL
(pages 372–383)

This section explains how to calculate the wavelength, frequency, or energy of light, given two of these values. It also explains the origin of the atomic emission spectrum of an element.

▶ Light and Atomic Spectra (pages 372–375)

1. Light consists of electromagnetic waves. What kinds of visible and invisible radiation are included in the electromagnetic spectrum?

_____

_____

_____

© Prentice-Hall, Inc.

2. Match each term describing waves to its definition.

_____ amplitude   **a.** the distance between two crests

_____ wavelength   **b.** the wave's height from the origin to the crest

_____ frequency   **c.** the number of wave cycles to pass a given point per unit of time

3. Label the parts of a wave in this drawing. Label the wavelength, the amplitude, the crest, and the origin.

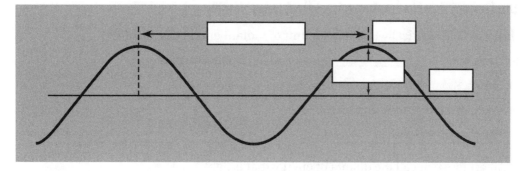

4. Is the following sentence true or false? The frequency and wavelength of all waves are inversely related. _____

5. The product of frequency and wavelength always equals a(n)

_____ , the speed of light.

6. The units of frequency are usually cycles per second. The SI unit of cycles per second is called a(n) _____ .

7. When sunlight passes through a prism, the different wavelengths separate into

a(n) _____ of colors.

8. Put the visible colors in order from light with the longest wavelength and lowest frequency to light with the shortest wavelength and the highest frequency.

_____ orange   _____ yellow

_____ green   _____ indigo

_____ blue   _____ red

_____ violet

9. Look at Figure 13.10 on page 373. The electromagnetic spectrum consists of radiation over a broad band of wavelengths. What type of radiation has the lowest frequency? The highest frequency?

_____

10. What happens when an electric discharge is passed through the gas or vapor of an element?

_____

CHAPTER 13, Electrons in Atoms *(continued)*

11. Passing the light emitted by an element through a prism gives the

_____ of the element.

12. Is the following sentence true or false? The emission spectrum of an element can be the same as the emission spectrum of another element.

_____

▶ The Quantum Concept and the Photoelectric Effect (pages 376–379)

13. Planck showed mathematically that the amount of radiant energy (E) absorbed

or emitted by a body is _____ to the frequency of the

radiation: $E = h \times v$.

14. What is a small, discrete unit of energy called?

_____

15. What did Albert Einstein call the quanta of energy that is light?

_____

16. What is the photoelectric effect?

_____

_____

17. Is the following sentence true or false? Albert Einstein recognized that there

is a threshold value of energy below which the photoelectric effect does not

occur. _____

▶ An Explanation of Atomic Spectra (pages 379–380)

18. What is the lowest energy level of an electron called? _____

19. Only electrons in transition from _____ to

_____ energy levels lose energy and emit light.

▶ Quantum Mechanics (pages 381–382)

20. What does de Broglie's equation describe?

_____

21. What does de Broglie's equation predict?

_____

22. Is the following sentence true or false? The new method of describing the

motions of subatomic particles, atoms, and molecules is called quantum

mechanics. _____

MathWise

GUIDED PRACTICE PROBLEM 11 (page 375)

11. What is the wavelength of radiation with a frequency of $1.50 \times 10^{13} \ s^{-1}$? Does this radiation have a longer or shorter wavelength than red light?

Analyze

Step 1. What is the equation for the relationship between frequency and wavelength? _____

Step 2. What does c represent and what is its value?

_____

Step 3. What is the wavelength of red light in cm?

_____

_____

Solve

Step 4. Solve the equation for the unknown. $\lambda =$ _____

Step 5. Substitute the known quantities into the equation and solve.

$$\frac{3.00 \times 10^{10} \text{ cm/s}}{\boxed{}} = \boxed{}$$

Step 6. Compare the answer with the wavelength of red light. Does the given radiation have a wavelength longer or shorter than that of red light?

_____

_____

Evaluate

Step 7. Explain why you think your result makes sense?

_____

_____

Step 8. Are the units in your answer correct? How do you know?

_____

© Prentice-Hall, Inc.

14 CHEMICAL PERIODICITY

SECTION 14.1 CLASSIFICATION OF THE ELEMENTS (pages 391–396)

This section explains why you can infer the properties of an element based on the properties of other elements in the periodic table. It also describes the use of electron configurations to classify elements.

▶ The Periodic Table Revisited (page 391)

1. In 1871, Russian chemist _____ created the forerunner of the modern periodic table.

2. List four things, other than the name and symbol, one can discover about an element using the periodic table in Figure 14.2.

   a. _____

   b. _____

   c. _____

   d. _____

3. How can the periodic table be used to predict the properties of the elements?

   _____

   _____ .

▶ Classifying Elements by Electron Configuration (pages 391–396)

4. Is the following sentence true or false? The subatomic particles that play the most significant role in determining the physical and chemical properties of an element are its electrons. _____

5. Complete the table about classifying elements according to their electron configurations.

Category	Description of Electron Configuration	Group
Noble gases		
Representative elements		
	outermost *s* sublevel and nearby *d* sublevel contain electrons	Group B
	outermost *s* sublevel and nearby *f* sublevel contain electrons	Group B

CHAPTER 14, Chemical Periodicity *(continued)*

Match the category of elements with an element from that category.

_____ **6.** Noble gases   **a.** gallium

_____ **7.** Representative elements   **b.** nobelium

_____ **8.** Transition metals   **c.** argon

_____ **9.** Inner transition metals   **d.** vanadium

10. Circle the letter of the elements found in the *p* block.

    a. Groups 1A and 2A and helium

    b. Groups 3A, 4A, 5A, 6A, 7A, and 0 except for helium

    c. transition metals

    d. inner transition metals

11. How many electrons can each type of orbital sublevel contain?

_____

_____

_____

12. Use Figure 14.5 on page 395. Write the electron configurations for the following elements.

    a. magnesium _____

    b. cobalt _____

    c. sulfur _____

SECTION 14.2 PERIODIC TRENDS (pages 398–406)

This section explains how to interpret group trends and periodic trends in atomic radii, ionic radii, ionization energies, and electronegativities.

▶ Trends in Atomic Size (pages 398–401)

    1. Is the following sentence true or false? The radius of an atom can be measured

    directly. _____

    2. What are the atomic radii for the following diatomic molecules?

      Hydrogen   **Oxygen**   **Nitrogen**   **Chlorine**

    atomic radius =   atomic radius =   atomic radius =   atomic radius =

    _____   _____   _____   _____

3. Use Figure 14.8 on page 399. What trend do you see in the sizes of elements within a group? Within a period?

_____

_____

4. What is the name of the effect that is responsible for differences in atomic radii between elements in the same group? _____

5. Number the following elements according to relative size from largest (1) to smallest (4).

_____ P

_____ He

_____ Ca

_____ Cs

▶ Trends in Ionization Energy (pages 401–403)

6. _____ is the energy required to overcome the attraction of the nuclear charge and remove an electron from a gaseous atom.

7. Why does ionization energy increase as you move across a period, but decrease as you move down a group?

_____

_____ .

_____

8. Suppose there is a large increase in energy between the second and the third ionization energies of a metal. What kind of ion is the metal likely to form?

_____

▶ Trends in Ionic Size (pages 403–404)

9. Metallic elements easily form _____ ions; nonmetallic elements readily form _____ ions.

10. Circle the letter of the statement that is true about ion size.

   a. Cations are always smaller than the neutral atoms from which they form.

   b. Anions are always smaller than the neutral atoms from which they form.

   c. Within a period, cations with greater charge have larger ionic radii.

   d. Within a group, cations with greater atomic number have smaller ionic radii.

11. Which ion has the larger ionic radius: Ca^{2+} or Cl^-? _____

© Prentice-Hall, Inc.

CHAPTER 14, Chemical Periodicity *(continued)*

▶ Trends in Electronegativity (page 405)

12. What property of an element represents its tendency to attract electrons when

    it chemically combines with another element? _____

13. Use Table 14.2 on page 405. What trend do you see in the relative
    electronegativity values of elements within a group? Within a period?

    _____

    _____

    _____

14. Circle the letter of each statement that is true about electronegativity values.

    a. The electronegativity values of the transition elements are all zero.

    b. The element with the highest electronegativity value is sodium.

    c. Nonmetals have higher electronegativity values than metals.

    d. Electronegativity values can help predict the types of bonds atoms form.

▶ Summary of Periodic Trends (page 406)

15. Use Figure 14.16 on page 406. Circle the letter of each property for which
    aluminum has a greater value than silicon.

    a. first ionization energy

    b. atomic radius

    c. electronegativity

    d. ionic radius

📖 Reading Skill Practice

A graph can help you understand comparisons of data at a glance. Use graph paper to make a graph
of the data in Table 14.2 on page 405. The vertical axis of your graph should represent electronegativity values and range from 0 to 4. The horizontal axis should represent atomic number. Label
each period and the first element in each period.

MathWise

GUIDED PRACTICE PROBLEM 1 (page 396)

1. Use Figure 14.5 to write the electron configurations of these elements.

    a. carbon   **b.** vanadium   **c.** strontium

Analyze

    a. What is the number of electrons for each element?

      C _____   V _____   Sr _____

    b. What is the highest occupied energy sublevel for each element, according to its position on the periodic table? Remember that the energy level for the *d* block is always one less than the period.

      C _____   V _____   Sr _____

    c. According to its position on the periodic table, how many electrons does each element have in the sublevel listed above?

      C _____   V _____   Sr _____

Calculate

    d. Begin filling in electron sublevels. Start from the top left and move right across each period in Figure 14.5 until you reach the highest occupied sublevel for each element. Make sure the *d*-block is in the correct energy level.

      C _____   V _____

      Sr _____

Evaluate

    e. How can you check whether your answers are correct?

      _____

      _____

    f. Check your answers as outlined above.

      C _____

      V _____

      Sr _____

EXTRA PRACTICE (similar to Practice Problem 2, page 396)

2. What are the symbols for all the elements that have outer configurations of s^2p^1?

_____

15 IONIC BONDING AND IONIC COMPOUNDS

SECTION 15.1 ELECTRON CONFIGURATION IN IONIC BONDING (pages 413–418)

This section explains how to use the periodic table to infer the number of valence electrons in an atom and draw its electron dot structure. It also describes the formation of cations from metals and anions from nonmetals.

▶ **Valence Electrons** (pages 413–414)

1. What are valence electrons? _____

    _____

2. The valence electrons largely determine the _____ of an

    element and are usually the only electrons used in _____ .

3. Is the following sentence true or false? The group number of an element in the

    periodic table is related to the number of valence electrons it has. _____

4. What is an electron dot structure? _____

    _____

5. Draw the electron dot structure of each of the following atoms.

    a. argon   _____

    b. calcium _____

    c. iodine _____

▶ **Electron Configurations for Cations** (pages 414–416)

6. What is the octet rule? _____

    _____

    _____

7. Metallic atoms tend to lose their valence electrons to produce a(n) _____,

    or a positively charged ion. Most nonmetallic atoms achieve a complete octet by

    gaining or _____ electrons.

CHAPTER 15, Ionic Bonding and Ionic Compounds *(continued)*

8. Write the electron configurations for these metals and circle the electrons lost when each metal forms a cation.

a. Mg _____

b. Al _____

c. K _____

Match the noble gas with its electron configuration.

_____ **9.** argon   **a.** $1s^2$

_____ **10.** helium   **b.** $1s^2 2s^2 2p^6$

_____ **11.** neon   **c.** $1s^2 2s^2 2p^6 3s^2 3p^6$

_____ **12.** krypton   **d.** $1s^2 2s^2 2p^6 3s^2 3p^6 3d^{10} 4s^2 4p^6$

13. What is the electron configuration called that has 18 electrons in the outer energy level and all of the orbitals filled?

_____

14. Write the electron configuration for zinc.

_____

15. Fill in the electron configuration diagram for the copper(I) ion.

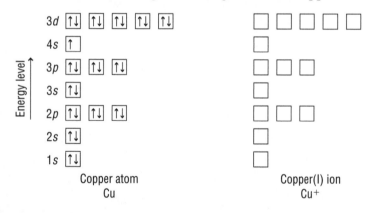

Copper atom
Cu

Copper(I) ion
Cu⁺

► Electron Configurations for Anions *(pages 417–418)*

16. Atoms of most nonmetallic elements achieve noble-gas electron

configurations by gaining electrons to become _____ , or

negatively charged ions.

17. What property of nonmetallic elements makes them more likely to gain electrons than lose electrons?

_____

18. Is the following sentence true or false? Elements of the halogen family lose one electron to become halide ions. _____

19. How many electrons will each element gain in forming an ion?

    a. nitrogen _____

    b. oxygen _____

    c. sulfur _____

    d. bromine _____

20. Write the symbol and electron configuration for each ion from Question 19, and name the noble gas with the same configuration.

    a. nitride _____

    b. oxide _____

    c. sulfide _____

    d. bromide _____

SECTION 15.2 IONIC BONDS (pages 419–425)

This section lists the characteristics of an ionic bond. It also describes the use of these characteristics to explain the electrical conductivity of ionic compounds when melted and when in aqueous solutions.

▶ Formation of Ionic Compounds (pages 419–421)

1. What is an ionic bond? _____

_____

2. In an ionic compound, the charges of the _____ and _____ must balance to produce an electrically _____ substance.

3. Complete the electron dot structures below to show how beryllium fluoride (BeF_2) is formed. Use Figure 15.7 on page 419 as a model.

$$F \qquad\qquad\qquad F$$

$$Be\ + \qquad\qquad \longrightarrow\ Be$$

$$F \qquad\qquad\qquad F$$

© Prentice-Hall, Inc.

CHAPTER 15, Ionic Bonding and Ionic Compounds *(continued)*

4. Why do beryllium and fluorine combine in a 1 : 2 ratio?

_____

_____

_____

▶ Properties of Ionic Compounds (pages 422–425)

5. Most ionic compounds are _____ at room temperature.

6. Is the following sentence true or false? Ionic compounds generally have low melting points. _____

7. What does a coordination number tell you?

_____

_____

8. What is the coordination number of the ions in a face-centered cubic crystal? In a simple cubic crystal? _____

9. Circle the letter of each statement that is true about ionic compounds.

a. The pattern of ions in a crystal structure can be determined by x-ray diffraction crystallography.

b. When melted, ionic compounds do not conduct electricity.

c. Ionic compounds do not dissolve in water.

d. The shape of a crystal depends on its unit cell structure.

Reading Skill Practice

By looking carefully at photographs and drawings in textbooks, you can better understand what you have read. Look carefully at Figure 15.8 on page 422. What important idea does this drawing communicate? Do your work on a separate sheet of paper.

SECTION 15.3 BONDING IN METALS (pages 427–429)

This section uses the theory of metallic bonds to explain the physical properties of metals. It also describes the arrangements of atoms in some common metallic crystal structures.

▶ Metallic Bonds and Metallic Properties (page 427)

1. Is the following sentence true or false? Metals are made up of cations, not

neutral atoms. _____

2. What are metallic bonds? _____

_____

_____

3. Name three properties of metals that can be explained by metallic bonding.

a. _____

b. _____

c. _____

4. What happens to an ionic crystal when a force is applied to it?

_____

_____

▶ Crystalline Structure of Metals (page 428)

5. Metal atoms in crystals are arranged into very _____ and orderly patterns.

6. Label each of the following arrangements of atoms with the correct name.

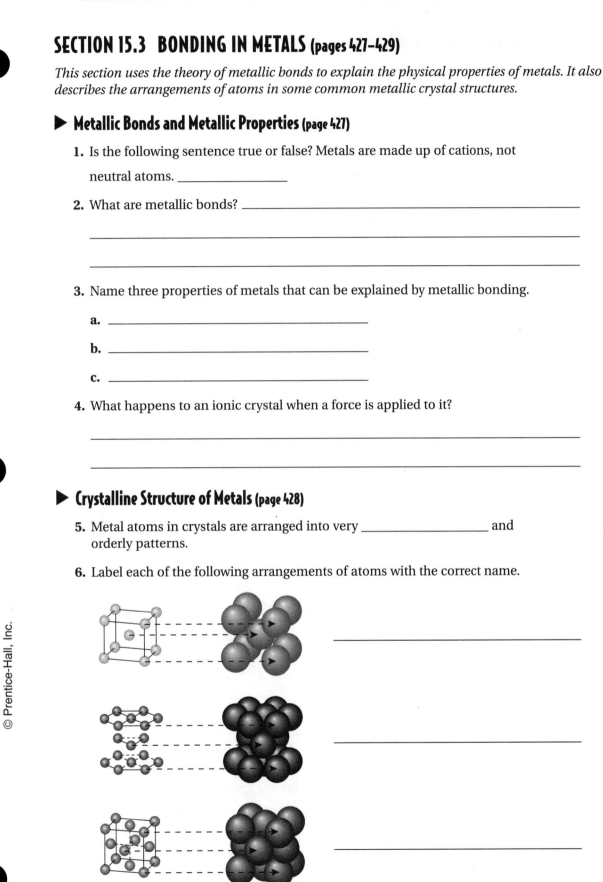

_____

_____

_____

CHAPTER 15, Ionic Bonding and Ionic Compounds *(continued)*

7. Circle the letter of each metal whose atoms form a face-centered cubic pattern.

   a. magnesium   **c.** sodium

   b. copper   **d.** aluminum

Match the arrangement with the number of neighbors each atom in the arrangement has.

_____ **8.** body-centered cubic   **a.** 12

_____ **9.** face-centered cubic   **b.** 8

_____ **10.** hexagonal close-packed

▶ Alloys (page 429)

11. A mixture of two or more elements, at least one of which is a metal, is called

    a(n) _____ .

12. Is the following sentence true or false? Pure metals are usually harder and

    more durable than alloys. _____

13. The most common use of nonferrous alloys is in _____ .

14. What four properties make steel an important alloy?

    a. _____

    b. _____

    c. _____

    d. _____

15. What are the component elements for the following alloys?

    a. sterling silver   _____

    b. brass   _____

    c. surgical steel   _____

    d. cast iron   _____

    e. dental amalgam _____

16. _____ alloys have smaller atoms that fit into the spaces between

    larger atoms. _____ alloys have component atoms that are

    roughly equal in size.

MathWise

GUIDED PRACTICE PROBLEM 8 (page 421)

8. Name the ionic compounds formed when the following elements combine:

a. potassium and iodine

Analyze

Step 1. Is the compound binary or ternary? _____

Step 2. Is one of the elements a metal? If so, which one?

_____

Calculate

Step 3. The name of the metal ion is the same as the name of the atom.

Remember that the nonmetal ion has an *-ide* ending. _____

Evaluate

Step 4. How do you know your answer is correct?

_____

_____

_____

b. aluminum and oxygen

Analyze

Step 1. Is the compound binary or ternary? _____

Step 2. Is one of the elements a metal? If so, which one?

_____

Calculate

Step 3. Name the metal ion the same as the atom. Name the compound.

_____

Evaluate

Step 4. How do you know your answer is correct?

_____

_____

© Prentice-Hall, Inc.

16 COVALENT BONDING

SECTION 16.1 THE NATURE OF COVALENT BONDING (pages 437–451)

This section uses electron dot structures to show the formation of single, double, and triple covalent bonds. It also describes and gives examples of coordinate covalent bonding, resonance structures, and exceptions to the octet rule.

▶ Single Covalent Bonds (pages 437–440)

1. What is a covalent bond?

   _____

2. Is the following sentence true or false? A shared pair of electrons is represented

   by a double dash. _____

3. Structural formulas show the arrangement of _____
   in molecules and polyatomic ions.

4. What is the octet rule of covalent bonding?

   _____

   _____

5. Use the electron dot diagram below. Circle each unshared pair of electrons in a
   water molecule.

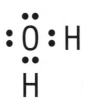

6. Complete the electron dot structure for each molecule. Each molecule
   contains only single covalent bonds.

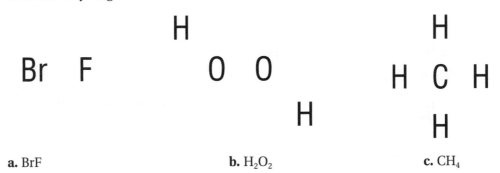

   a. BrF   **b.** H_2O_2 **c.** CH_4

© Prentice-Hall, Inc.

CHAPTER 16, Covalent Bonding *(continued)*

▶ Double and Triple Covalent Bonds *(pages 442–443)*

7. A chemical bond formed when atoms share two pairs of electrons is called a(n)

_____ .

8. Use Figure 16.5 on page 442. How many covalent bonds are in the nitrogen

molecule? _____

9. Is the following sentence true or false? All diatomic molecules contain double

bonds. _____

▶ Coordinate Covalent Bonds *(pages 444–447)*

10. What is a coordinate covalent bond?

_____

11. Look at Table 16.2 on page 445. Which three nitrogen compounds contain
coordinate covalent bonds?

_____

12. Complete the electron dot structure of the chlorate ion (ClO_3^-) by filling in the
bonds and unpaired electrons.

$$\left[\begin{array}{ccc} O & Cl - \overset{\bullet\bullet}{\underset{\bullet\bullet}{O}} \colon \\ & O & \end{array}\right]^-$$

▶ Bond Dissociation Energies *(pages 447–448)*

13. What is bond dissociation energy?

_____

_____

14. Is the following sentence true or false? Molecules with high bond dissociation

energies are relatively unreactive. _____

15. Use Table 16.3 on page 448. What are the bond energies for the following
covalent bonds?

    a. $C \equiv O$ _____

    b. $C - N$ _____

    c. $O - O$ _____

16. Circle the letter of the correct answer. How many kilojoules are required to dissociate all the bonds in 0.25 mole of carbon dioxide (CO_2)?

a. 736 kJ   **b.** 368 kJ   **c.** 184 kJ   **d.** 1472 kJ

▶ Resonance (page 449)

17. What are resonance structures?

_____

_____

18. The actual bonding in ozone is a _____ of the extremes

represented by its _____ .

▶ Exceptions to the Octet Rule (pages 449–451)

19. Why does NO_2 not follow the octet rule?

_____

20. Oxygen molecules are _____ because they contain unpaired electrons.

SECTION 16.2 BONDING THEORIES (pages 452–459)

This section describes the molecular orbital theory of covalent bonding, including orbital hybridization. It also explains the use of VSEPR theory to predict the shapes of some molecules.

▶ Molecular Orbitals (pages 452–455)

1. What is a molecular orbital?

_____

_____

2. What two molecular orbitals are created when two atomic orbitals overlap?

a. _____   **b.** _____

3. Is the following sentence true or false? Electrons fill the antibonding molecular orbital first to produce a stable covalent bond. _____

4. When two *s* atomic orbitals combine, the molecular orbital formed is called a(n) _____ bond.

5. For a stable covalent bond to form, the _____ between the nuclei and the electrons must be stronger than the _____ .

6. Circle the letter of each type of covalent bond that can be formed when *p* atomic orbitals overlap.

a. pi   **b.** beta   **c.** sigma   **d.** alpha

CHAPTER 16, Covalent Bonding *(continued)*

▶ VSEPR Theory (pages 455–457)

7. What is VSEPR theory?

_____

_____

8. When the central atom of a molecule has unshared electrons, the bond angles will be _____ than when all the central atom's electrons are shared.

9. What is the bond angle in carbon dioxide? Why?

_____

10. What are the names of these common molecular shapes?

_____

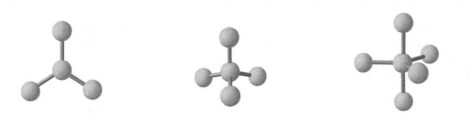

_____

▶ Hybrid Orbitals (pages 457–459)

11. What is orbital hybridization?

_____

_____

12. Is the following sentence true or false? Orbital hybridization theory can describe both the shape and bonding of molecules. _____

Match the hybrid orbitals formed by carbon with the carbon compound in which they are found.

_____ **13.** sp^3 **a.** ethyne

_____ **14.** sp^2 **b.** ethene

_____ **15.** sp **c.** methane

Reading Skill Practice

You can increase your understanding of what you have read by making comparisons. A compare/contrast table can help you do this. On a separate sheet of paper, draw a table to compare the three types of hybrid orbitals as explained on pages 458 and 459. The three heads for the rows should be *sp, sp²*, and *sp³*. Then list the characteristics that will form the basis of your comparison above each column. The column heads should be *Number of Hybrid Orbitals, Component Orbitals, Number of Bonds,* and *Bond Angle.*

SECTION 16.3 POLAR BONDS AND MOLECULES (pages 460–466)

This section explains the use of electronegativity values to classify a bond as nonpolar covalent, polar covalent, or ionic. It also names and describes the weak attractive forces that hold groups of molecules together.

▶ Bond Polarity (pages 460–462)

1. Is the following statement true or false? Covalent bonds differ in the way electrons are shared by the bonded atoms, depending on the kind and number of atoms joined together. _____

2. Describe how electrons are shared in each type of bond. Write *equally* or *unequally.*

   a. Nonpolar bond _____   **b.** Polar bond _____

3. Why does the chlorine atom in hydrogen chloride acquire a slightly negative charge? _____

   _____

4. What symbols are used to represent the charges on atoms in a polar covalent bond? The polarity of the bond? _____

Match the electronegativity difference range with the most probable type of bond that will form.

_____ **5.** 0.0–0.4   **a.** ionic

_____ **6.** 0.4–1.0   **b.** nonpolar covalent

_____ **7.** 1.0–2.0   **c.** very polar covalent

_____ **8.** > 2.0   **d.** moderately polar covalent

CHAPTER 16, Covalent Bonding *(continued)*

▶ Polar Molecules (pages 462–463)

9. Circle the letter of each sentence that is true about polar molecules.

a. Some regions of a polar molecule are slightly negative and some are slightly positive.

b. A molecule containing a polar bond is always polar.

c. A molecule that has two poles is called a dipolar molecule.

d. When polar molecules are placed in an electric field, they all line up with the same orientation in relation to the charged plates.

10. Are the following molecules polar or nonpolar?

a. H_2O _____   **c.** NH_3 _____

b. CO_2 _____   **d.** CCl _____

▶ Attractions Between Molecules (pages 463–465)

11. What causes the two types of van der Waals forces?

_____

_____

12. Is the following sentence true or false? Dispersion forces generally increase in strength as the number of electrons in a molecule increases. _____

13. The strongest of the intermolecular forces are _____ .

▶ Intermolecular Attractions and Molecular Properties (pages 465–466)

14. What determines the physical properties of a compound?

_____

15. Use Table 16.5 on page 465. Complete the following table comparing ionic and covalent compounds.

Characteristic	Ionic Compound	Covalent Compound
Representative unit		
Physical state		
Melting point		
Solubility in water		

MathWise

GUIDED PRACTICE PROBLEM 19 (page 462)

19. Identify the bonds between atoms of each pair of elements as nonpolar covalent, moderately polar covalent, very polar covalent, or ionic.

   a. H and Br   **b.** K and Cl   **c.** O and O   **d.** Br and F

Analyze

Step 1. What is the most probable type of bond for each electronegativity difference range?

Electronegativity Difference Range	Most Probable Type of Bond
0.0–0.4	_____
0.4–1.0	_____
1.0–2.0	_____
≥ 2.0	_____

Calculate

Step 2. From Table 14.2 on page 405, determine the electronegativity values and differences for each pair of elements.

a. H = 2.1, Br = [＿＿＿]; difference = [＿＿＿]

b. K = [＿＿＿], Cl = 3.0; difference = [＿＿＿]

c. O = [＿＿＿], O = 3.5; difference = [＿＿＿]

d. Br = 2.8, F = [＿＿＿]; difference = [＿＿＿]

Step 3. Refer to Table 16.4 on page 462 to determine the most probable type of bond for each compound.

   a. _____

   b. _____

   c. _____

   d. _____

Evaluate

Step 4. How do you know that your answers are correct?

_____

_____

17 WATER AND AQUEOUS SYSTEMS

SECTION 17.1 LIQUID WATER AND ITS PROPERTIES (pages 475–478)

This section explains the hydrogen bonding that occurs in water molecules and how high surface tension and low vapor pressure can be explained in terms of hydrogen bonding.

▶ The Water Molecule (pages 475–476)

1. What unique molecular compound is the foundation of all life on Earth?

   _____

2. Approximately what fraction of Earth's surface is covered in water? _____

3. Circle the letter next to each sentence that is true concerning water molecules.

   a. Each O — H covalent bond in a water molecule is nonpolar.

   b. In a water molecule, the less electronegative hydrogen atoms acquire a slight positive charge and the oxygen atom acquires a slight negative charge.

   c. Because the water molecule has an H — O — H bond angle of 105°, the molecule as a whole is polar.

4. The diagram below depicts a water molecule. Complete the labels showing the locations of the hydrogen atoms, the oxygen atom, and the regions of positive and negative charge.

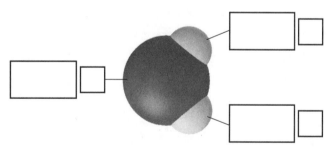

5. List five important properties of water that result from hydrogen bonding.

   a. _____

   b. _____

   c. _____

   d. _____

   e. _____

CHAPTER 17, Water and Aqueous Systems *(continued)*

6. The diagram below depicts a collection of water molecules. Draw dotted lines showing where hydrogen bonding occurs.

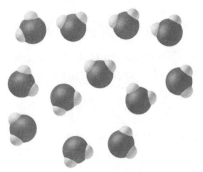

▶ Surface Properties (pages 476–477)

7. Circle the letter next to each sentence that describes a result of the surface tension of water.

   a. In a full glass of water, the water surface seems to bulge over the rim of the glass.

   b. Water beads up into small, nearly spherical drops on a paper towel.

   c. Water forms nearly spherical drops at the end of an eyedropper.

   d. An insect called a water strider is able to "walk" on water.

8. Using Figure 17.5 on page 477, explain why a water drop has surface tension.

   _____

   _____

   _____

9. What geometric shape has the smallest surface area for a given volume?

   _____

10. Circle the letter next to each sentence that correctly describes a property of detergents.

   a. Detergent molecules interfere with hydrogen bonding between water molecules.

   b. Detergent molecules strengthen hydrogen bonding between water molecules.

   c. Detergents act as "wetting agents."

   d. When detergents reduce surface tension, beads of water collapse and the water spreads out.

© Prentice-Hall, Inc.

11. Do liquids that have higher surface tension produce drops that are flatter or more nearly spherical than liquids with lower surface tension?

_____

_____

12. What is the name for an agent, such as a detergent, that has the ability to

reduce surface tension? _____

▶ Specific Heat Capacity (page 478)

13. The high specific heat capacity of water is due to _____
bonding.

14. Is the following sentence true or false? Iron requires nearly 10 times more heat than an equal mass of liquid water to produce the same temperature increase.

_____

15. What effect does a large body of water have on the daily temperature of the air around it?

_____

_____

SECTION 17.2 WATER VAPOR AND ICE (pages 479–481)

This section explains why water has a high heat of vaporization and a high boiling point. It also explains why ice floats on liquid water.

▶ Evaporation and Condensation (pages 479–480)

1. Is the following sentence true or false? Because of hydrogen bonding, water absorbs a large amount of heat as it evaporates or vaporizes.

_____

2. Circle the letter next to each sentence that is true about vaporization or condensation of water.

a. An extensive network of hydrogen bonds tightly holds the molecules in liquid water together.

b. Hydrogen bonds continue to exist between water molecules in the vapor state.

c. Because liquid methane has no hydrogen bonding, its heat of vaporization is higher than that of water.

d. The amount of heat given off during the condensation of one gram of water is the same as the amount of heat absorbed by one gram of water when it vaporizes.

CHAPTER 17, Water and Aqueous Systems *(continued)*

3. How are the evaporation and condensation of water important to regional

temperatures on Earth? _____

_____

_____

_____

4. Look at Table 17.1 on page 480, which shows several substances with low

molar mass. What is unusual about the boiling point of water? How can this

difference be explained? _____

_____

_____

▶ Ice (pages 480–481)

5. What happens to the density of most substances as they cool and solidify?

_____

_____

6. The diagrams below show hydrogen bonding in water molecules.

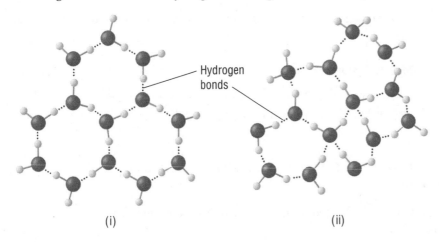

(i)   (ii)

a. Which diagram depicts ice? _____

b. Which diagram depicts liquid water? _____

c. Why is ice less dense than liquid water? Refer to the diagrams to help you

explain. _____

_____

_____

© Prentice-Hall, Inc.

7. Look at Table 17.2 on page 480. To four significant figures, list the density of

    a. liquid water at 4 °C _____

    b. liquid water at 0 °C _____

    c. ice at 0 °C   _____

8. What is unusual about the data in Question 7? Will ice float on liquid water?

_____

_____

_____

SECTION 17.3 AQUEOUS SOLUTIONS (pages 482–488)

This section describes the process of solvation; distinguishes among strong electrolytes, weak electrolytes, and nonelectrolytes; and explains water of hydration.

▶ Solvents and Solutes (page 482)

1. Water samples containing dissolved substances are called

    _____ .

Match each term to its description by writing its letter on the line next to the description.

_____ **2.** dissolving medium   **a.** solution

_____ **3.** dissolved particles   **b.** solute

_____ **4.** homogeneous mixture of particles in a   **c.** solvent
                  dissolving medium

5. Is the following sentence true or false? After sodium chloride dissolves in a container of water, the sodium chloride will eventually settle to the bottom of the container if the solution remains undisturbed at a constant temperature.

_____

6. Circle the letter next to each sentence that is true about aqueous solutions.

    a. Solute particles can be either ionic or molecular, and their average diameters are usually less than 1.0 nanometers.

    b. When a solution is filtered, both solute and solvent will pass through the filter paper.

    c. Ionic compounds and substances containing polar covalent molecules readily dissolve in water.

    d. Nonpolar covalent molecules, such as those found in oil, grease, and gasoline, readily dissolve in water.

CHAPTER 17, Water and Aqueous Systems *(continued)*

7. Is the following sentence true or false? Solvents and solutes may be gases, liquids, or solids. _____

▶ **The Solution Process** (page 483)

8. When a solid crystal of sodium chloride is placed in water, what happens?

_____

9. What process occurs when solute ions become surrounded by solvent molecules? _____

10. Look at the model of solvation in Figure 17.12 on page 483. If there is enough solvent, what will eventually happen to the ionic solid depicted on the left side of the diagram?

_____

_____

11. When a compound cannot be solvated to any significant extent, it is called

_____ .

12. Circle the letter next to the one sentence that best explains why the ionic compounds barium sulfate ($BaSO_4$) and calcium carbonate ($CaCO_3$) are nearly insoluble in water.

   a. The attractions between the ions in the crystals of these ionic compounds are weaker than the attractions between the ions and water molecules.

   b. The attractions between the ions in the crystals of these ionic compounds are stronger than the attractions between the ions and water molecules.

   c. There is no difference in the strength of the attractions between the ions in the crystals and the attractions between the ions and water molecules.

   d. These ionic compounds are easily dissolved in water.

13. What saying sums up the observation that, as a rule, polar solvents dissolve ionic compounds and polar molecules, but nonpolar solvents dissolve nonpolar compounds? _____

▶ **Electrolytes and Nonelectrolytes** (pages 483–485)

14. What types of compounds can carry an electric current in the molten state or in aqueous solution? _____

15. Is the following sentence true or false? All ionic compounds are electrolytes.

_____

16. Compounds that do not conduct an electric current in either aqueous solution or the molten state are called _____ .

Look at the light bulbs in Figure 17.14 on page 484 to answer Questions 17, 18, and 19.

_____ **17.** Which bulb, *a*, *b*, or *c*, indicates that the solution is nonconductive?

_____ **18.** Which bulb, *a*, *b*, or *c*, indicates that the solution is weakly conductive?

_____ **19.** Which bulb, *a*, *b*, or *c*, indicates that the solution is highly conductive?

▶ **Water of Hydration (pages 485–488)**

20. Water in a crystal that is an integral part of the crystal structure is called

_____ .

21. A compound that contains water as an integral part of its crystal structure is

called _____ .

22. What does "·5H$_2$O" mean when included in a chemical formula?

_____

23. Circle the letter next to each sentence that is true about hydrated compounds. Use Figures 17.15 and 17.16 on page 486 to help you.

a. Crystals of copper sulfate pentahydrate always contain five molecules of water for each copper and sulfate ion pair.

b. Heating blue crystals of copper sulfate pentahydrate above 100 °C drives off the water of hydration, leaving a white anhydrous powder.

c. It is possible to regenerate copper sulfate pentahydrate by treating anhydrous copper sulfate with water.

d. Anhydrous cobalt(II) chloride is a good indicator for the presence of water because it changes from pink to blue when exposed to moisture.

24. If a hydrate has a vapor pressure greater than that of the water in the

surrounding air, the hydrate will lose water to the air, or _____ .

25. Hygroscopic substances that remove water from the air are used as drying

agents called _____ .

26. Look at Figure 17.17 on page 487. What happens to dry sodium hydroxide pellets that are exposed to normally moist air? What kind of compound exhibits this behavior?

_____

_____

_____

CHAPTER 17, Water and Aqueous Systems *(continued)*

📖 Reading Skill Practice

By looking carefully at photographs and drawings in your textbook, you can better understand what you have read. Look carefully at Figure 17.13 on page 483. What important idea does this photograph communicate? Do your work on a separate sheet of paper.

SECTION 17.4 HETEROGENEOUS AQUEOUS SYSTEMS (pages 490–493)

This section describes how colloids and suspensions differ from solutions and explains the Tyndall effect.

▶ **Suspensions (page 490)**

1. Is the following sentence true or false? Heterogeneous mixtures are not true

   solutions. _____

2. Heterogeneous mixtures in which particles settle out upon standing are called

   _____ .

3. Is the following sentence true or false? When a suspension of clay particles in water is filtered, both clay and water will pass through the filter paper.

   _____

▶ **Colloids (pages 490–493)**

4. Heterogeneous mixtures in which particles are of intermediate size

   between those of true solutions and suspensions are called _____ .

5. The scattering of light in all directions by colloidal particles is known as the

   _____ .

6. Identify each type of system shown in the figure below.

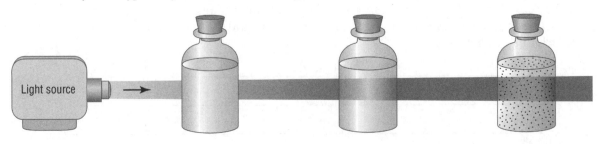

_____   _____   _____

MathWise

GUIDED PRACTICE PROBLEM 8 (page 488)

8. What is the percent by mass of water in $CuSO_4 \cdot 5H_2O$?

Analyze

a. What formula do you use to find percent by mass of water in a hydrate?

percent H_2O = $\dfrac{\boxed{}}{\boxed{}}$ × $\boxed{}$

b. From the periodic table, what is the average atomic mass of each of the following elements?

Cu = _____   O = _____

S = _____   H = _____

Calculate

c. Determine the mass of water in the hydrate.

mass of $5H_2O$ = 5 × [(2 × $\boxed{}$) + $\boxed{}$)] = 5 × $\boxed{}$ = $\boxed{}$ g

d. Determine the mass of the hydrate.

mass of $CuSO_4 \cdot H_2O$ = 63.5 + 32.1 + (4 × $\boxed{}$) + $\boxed{}$ = $\boxed{}$ g

e. Calculate the percent by mass of water.

percent H_2O = $\dfrac{\boxed{}}{\boxed{}}$ × 100% = $\boxed{}$ %

Evaluate

f. How do you know that your answer is correct?

_____

_____

EXTRA PRACTICE (similar to Practice Problem 8, page 488)

8. What is the percent by mass of water in $CaCl_2 \cdot 2H_2O$?

18 **SOLUTIONS**

SECTION 18.1 PROPERTIES OF SOLUTIONS (pages 501–508)

This section identifies the factors that affect the solubility of a substance and determine the rate at which a solute dissolves.

▶ **Solution Formation** (pages 501–502)

Look at Figure 18.1 on page 501 to help you answer Questions 1 and 2.

1. What does the picture of the sugar cube suspended in water tell you about where on a solid sample the solution process takes place?

_____

2. Underline the condition that causes sugar to dissolve *faster* in water.

   a. as a whole cube   or   in granulated form?

   b. when allowed to stand   or   when stirred?

   c. at a higher temperature or   a lower temperature?

3. Name three factors that influence the rate at which a solute dissolves in a solvent.

   a. _____

   b. _____

   c. _____

4. Is the following sentence true or false? Finely ground particles dissolve more rapidly than larger particles because finer particles expose a greater surface area to the colliding solvent molecules. _____

▶ **Solubility** (pages 502–503)

5. Complete the following table showing the steps in a procedure to determine the total amount of sodium chloride that will dissolve in 100 g of water at 25 °C.

Procedure	Amount Dissolved	Amount Not Dissolved
Add 36.0 g of sodium chloride to the water	36.0 g	0.0 g
Add an additional 1.0 g of sodium chloride		
Determine the total amount that dissolves		

CHAPTER 18, Solutions *(continued)*

6. The amount of a substance that dissolves in a given quantity of solvent at a constant temperature is called the substance's _____ .

7. If a solution contains the *maximum* amount of solute for a given quantity of solvent at a constant temperature, it is called a(n) _____ solution.

8. Look at Figure 18.2 on page 503. Circle the letter of each sentence that is true about a saturated solution.

   a. The total amount of dissolved solute remains constant.

   b. The total mass of undissolved crystals remains constant.

   c. When the rate of solvation equals the rate of crystallization, a state of dynamic equilibrium exists.

   d. If more solute were added to the container, the total amount of dissolved solute would increase.

9. If two liquids dissolve each other, they are said to be _____ .

10. Look at Figure 18.3 on page 503. Why does the oil float on the vinegar?

_____

_____

▶ Factors Affecting Solubility (pages 503–507)

11. Is the following sentence true or false? The solubility of sodium chloride in water increases to 39.2 g per 100 g of water at 100 °C from 36.2 g per 100 g of water at 25 °C. _____

12. Circle the letter of the sentence that best answers the following question. How does the solubility of solid substances change as the temperature of the solvent increases?

   a. The solubility increases for all solids.

   b. The solubility increases for most solids.

   c. The solubility remains constant.

13. Look at Table 18.1 on page 504. Which solid substance listed in the table is nearly insoluble at any temperature? _____

14. How does the solubility of a gas change with an increase in temperature?

_____

15. The directly proportional relationship between the solubility of a gas in a liquid and the pressure of the gas above the liquid is known as

_____ .

16. Describe the two diagrams of a bottled carbonated beverage below as *greater pressure* or *less pressure,* and then as *greater solubility* or *less solubility.* How do these two examples illustrate the relationship between the solubility of a gas and its vapor pressure?

_____

_____

_____

_____   _____

17. How does a solution become supersaturated? _____

_____

_____

_____

SECTION 18.2 CONCENTRATIONS OF SOLUTIONS (pages 509–515)

This section explains how to solve problems involving molarity of a solution, how to prepare dilute solutions from more concentrated solutions, and what is meant by percent by volume and percent by mass.

▶ Molarity (pages 509–511)

1. A measure of the amount of solute dissolved in a given quantity of solvent is

the _____ of a solution.

2. The most important unit of concentration in chemistry is _____ .

3. Is the following sentence true or false? Molarity is the number of moles of

dissolved solute per liter of solvent. _____

CHAPTER 18, Solutions *(continued)*

4. Look at Figure 18.10 on page 509. Circle the letter of the best procedure for making a 0.50-molar (0.50*M*) solution in a 1.0-L volumetric flask.

a. Add distilled water exactly to the 1.0-L mark, add 0.50 mol of solute, and then agitate to dissolve the solute.

b. Place 0.50 mol of solute in the flask, add distilled water to the 1.0-L mark, and then agitate to dissolve the solute.

c. Combine 0.50 mol of water with 0.50 mol of solute in the flask, and then agitate to dissolve the solute.

d. Fill the flask with distilled water until it is about half full, add 0.50 mol of solute, agitate to dissolve the solute, and then carefully fill the flask with distilled water to the 1.0-L mark.

5. List the information needed to find the molarity of a 2.0-L solution containing 0.50 mol of sodium chloride.

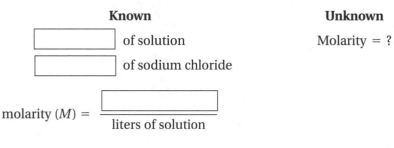

Known	**Unknown**
⬚ of solution	Molarity = ?
⬚ of sodium chloride	

$$\text{molarity } (M) = \frac{\boxed{}}{\text{liters of solution}}$$

▶ Making Dilutions (pages 511–513)

6. How do you make a solution less concentrated? _____

7. On the diagram below, assume that each beaker contains an equal number of moles of solute. Label each solution as *concentrated* or *dilute*. Then indicate the approximate relative volumes of each solution by drawing in the surface level on each beaker.

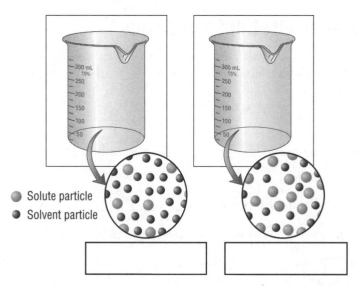

● Solute particle
● Solvent particle

Questions 8 and 9 refer to the following situation. Solvent is added to a solution until the total volume of the solution doubles.

8. What happens to the number of moles of solute present in the solution when the volume doubles?

_____

9. Circle the letter of the correct description of the change in molarity of a solution when the volume doubles.

a. The molarity of the solution is cut in half.

b. The molarity of the solution doubles.

c. The molarity of the solution remains constant.

d. The molarity of the solution increases slightly.

10. List the information you need to find how many milliliters of a stock solution of $2.00M$ $MgSO_4$ you would need to prepare 100.0 mL of $1.00M$ $MgSO_4$.

Known	Unknown
M_1 = _____	V_1 = ? mL of $2.00M$ $MgSO_4$
M_2 = _____	
V_2 = _____	
$M_1 \times$ _____ = _____ $\times$ _____	

▶ **Percent Solutions** (pages 513–515)

11. List the information needed to find the percent by volume of ethanol in a solution when 50 mL of pure ethanol is diluted with water to a volume of 250 mL.

Known	Unknown
Volume of ethanol = _____	% ethanol by volume = ? %
Volume of solution = _____	

% (v/v) = _____

📖 Reading Skill Practice

Writing a summary can help you remember the information you have read. When you write a summary, include only the most important points. Write a summary of the information about percent solutions on pages 513–514. Your summary should be shorter than the text on which it is based. Do your work on a separate sheet of paper.

CHAPTER 18, Solutions *(continued)*

SECTION 18.3 COLLIGATIVE PROPERTIES OF SOLUTIONS (pages 517–519)

This section explains why a solution has a lower vapor pressure, an elevated boiling point, and a depressed freezing point compared with the pure solvent of that solution.

▶ **Decrease in Vapor Pressure (pages 517–518)**

1. Properties of a solution that depend only on the number of particles

   dissolved, but not the identity of solute particles in the solution are called

   _____ .

2. Is the following sentence true or false? A nonvolatile substance is one that does

   not vaporize easily. _____

3. Look at Figure 18.15 on page 517. What happens to the vapor pressure equilibrium when a nonvolatile solute is added to a pure solvent?

   _____

   _____

4. How is the decrease in vapor pressure in a solution with a nonvolatile solute related to the number of particles per formula unit of solute?

   _____

   _____

   _____

5. Assume 3 mol each of three different solutes have been added to three identical beakers of water as shown below. If the beakers are covered to form closed systems at constant temperature, rank the vapor pressures in each container from 1 (lowest) to 3 (highest).

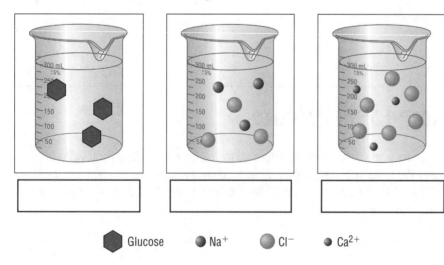

⬡ Glucose   🔴 Na⁺   ⚪ Cl⁻   🔴 Ca²⁺

▶ Boiling-Point Elevation (pages 518–519)

6. Circle the letter next to each sentence that is true concerning the boiling point of a solution formed by a liquid solvent and a nonvolatile solute.

    a. The boiling point is the temperature at which the vapor pressure equals atmospheric pressure.

    b. Adding a nonvolatile solute decreases the vapor pressure.

    c. Because of the decrease in vapor pressure, additional kinetic energy must be added to raise the vapor pressure of the liquid phase to atmospheric pressure.

    d. The boiling point of the solution is higher than the boiling point of the pure solvent.

7. The difference between the boiling point of a solution and that of the pure

    solvent is called the _____ .

▶ Freezing-Point Depression (page 519)

8. Circle the letter of each sentence that is true about the freezing point of a solution formed by a liquid solvent and nonvolatile solute.

    a. When a substance freezes, the arrangement of its particles becomes less orderly.

    b. The presence of a solute in water disrupts the formation of orderly patterns as the solution is cooled to the freezing point of pure water.

    c. More kinetic energy must be withdrawn from a solution than from a pure solvent in order for the solution to solidify.

    d. The freezing point of the solution is lower than the freezing point of the pure solvent.

9. One mole of which substance, glucose or sodium chloride, will produce more freezing-point depression when added to equal amounts of water? Why?

    _____

    _____

SECTION 18.4 CALCULATIONS INVOLVING COLLIGATIVE PROPERTIES
(pages 520–525)

This section explains how to calculate the molality and mole fraction of a solution, and how to calculate the molar mass of a compound from the freezing-point depression or boiling-point elevation of a solution of the compound.

▶ Molality and Mole Fraction (pages 520–522)

1. For a solution, the ratio of moles of solute to mass of solvent in kilograms,

    represented by lower-case "*m*," is the solution's _____ .

CHAPTER 18, Solutions *(continued)*

2. Is the following sentence true or false? Molarity and molality are always the same for a solution. _____

3. What is the molality of a solution prepared by adding 1.0 mol of sodium chloride to 2.0 kg of water? _____

4. The pie chart below shows the ratio of ethylene glycol (EG) to water in one antifreeze solution. Write the mole fractions for each substance.

Mole fraction EG $= \dfrac{\boxed{}}{\boxed{} + \boxed{}} = \dfrac{\boxed{}}{\boxed{}} = \boxed{}$

Mole fraction $H_2O = \dfrac{\boxed{}}{\boxed{} + \boxed{}} = \dfrac{\boxed{}}{\boxed{}} = \boxed{}$

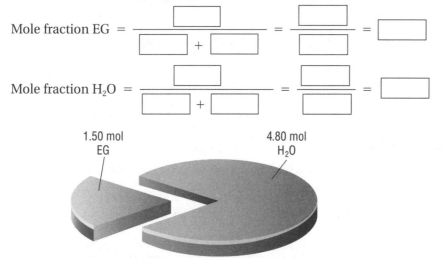

1.50 mol
EG

4.80 mol
H_2O

▶ Boiling-Point Elevation and Freezing-Point Depression *(pages 522–524)*

5. Assuming a solute is molecular and not ionic, the magnitude of the boiling-point elevation of the solution, ΔT_b, is directly proportional to

_____ .

6. Look at Table 18.2 on page 523. What is the molal boiling-point elevation constant, K_b, for water? _____

7. You need to find the freezing point of a $1.50m$ aqueous NaCl solution. You calculate ΔT_f to be $1.86\,°C/m \times 3.00m$ or $5.86\,°C$. What is the temperature at which the solution freezes? _____

▶ Molar Mass *(pages 524–525)*

8. Explain how you could use freezing-point depression to compute an unknown molar mass of a compound.

_____

_____

_____

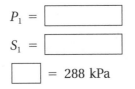

GUIDED PRACTICE PROBLEM 1 (page 507)

1. The solubility of a gas in water is 0.16 g/L at 104 kPa of pressure. What is the solubility when the pressure of the gas is increased to 288 kPa? Assume the temperature remains constant.

Analyze

Step 1. What is the equation for the relationship between solubility and

pressure? _____

Step 2. What is this law called? _____

Step 3. What are the known values in this problem?

$P_1 =$ [_____]

$S_1 =$ [_____]

[_____] $= 288$ kPa

Step 4. What is the unknown in this problem? _____

Solve

Step 5. Rearrange the equation to solve for the unknown.

$S_2 =$

Step 6. Substitute the known values into the equation and solve.

$$S_2 = \frac{[\qquad] \text{g/L} \times [\qquad] \text{kPa}}{[\qquad] \text{kPa}} = [\qquad]$$

Evaluate

Step 7. How do you know that your answer is correct?

_____

_____

Step 8. Are the units correct? Explain.

_____

_____

CHAPTER 18, Solutions *(continued)*

GUIDED PRACTICE PROBLEM 8 *(page 511)*

8. A solution has a volume of 2.0 L and contains 36.0 g of glucose. If the molar mass of glucose is 180 g/mol, what is the molarity of the solution?

_____

Step 1. What is the equation for molarity of a solution?

Molarity (M) = _____

Step 2. How many moles of glucose are in the solution?

$\boxed{}$ g $\times \dfrac{1 \text{ mol}}{\boxed{} \text{ g}} = \boxed{}$ mol glucose

Step 3. Substitute the known values into the equation for molarity.

$M = \dfrac{\boxed{}}{2.0 \ \boxed{}}$

Step 4. Solve.

$M =$ _____

EXTRA PRACTICE *(similar to Practice Problem 10, page 511)*

10. How many moles of ammonium nitrate are in 375 mL of $0.40M$ NH_4NO_3?

GUIDED PRACTICE PROBLEM 14 *(page 514)*

14. If 10 mL of pure acetone is diluted with water to a total solution volume of 200 mL, what is the percent by volume of acetone in the solution?

_____

Step 1. What is the equation for calculating percent by volume?

% (v/v) = _____ $\times$ 100%

Step 2. What are the knowns in this problem?

_____

_____

Step 3. Substitute the known values into the equation and solve.

% (v/v) = $\dfrac{\boxed{} \text{ mL}}{\boxed{} \text{ mL}} \times 100\% = \boxed{}$ %

EXTRA PRACTICE (similar to Practice Problem 30, page 522)

30. What is the mole fraction of each component in a solution made by mixing 230 g of ethanol (C_2H_5OH) and 450 g of water?

n_{ETH} = _____

n_{WAT} = _____

X_{ETH} = _____

X_{WAT} = _____

GUIDED PRACTICE PROBLEM 32 (page 524)

32. What is the boiling point of a solution that contains 1.25 mol $CaCl_2$ in 1400 g of water?

Step 1. What is the concentration of the $CaCl_2$ solution?	$\dfrac{1.25\ \text{mol}}{\boxed{}\ \text{g}} \times \dfrac{\boxed{}\ \text{g}}{1\ \text{kg}} = \boxed{}\ m$
Step 2. How many particles are produced by the ionization of each formula unit of $CaCl_2$?	$CaCl_2(s) \longrightarrow Ca^+ + \boxed{}\ Cl^-$, therefore _____ particles are produced.
Step 3. What is the total molality of the solution?	_____ $\times\ 0.89\ m\ =\ 2.7m$
Step 4. What is the molal boiling point elevation constant (K_b) for water?	K_b (water) = _____ °C/m
Step 5. Calculate the boiling point elevation.	ΔT_b = _____ °C/$m \times 2.7$ _____ = 1.4 _____
Step 6. Add ΔT_b to 100 °C to find the new boiling point.	_____ °C + 100 °C = _____ °C

19 REACTION RATES AND EQUILIBRIUM

SECTION 19.1 RATES OF REACTION (pages 533–538)

This section explains what is meant by the rate of a chemical reaction. It also uses collision theory to show how the rate of a chemical reaction is influenced by the reaction conditions.

▶ Collision Theory (pages 533–536)

1. How are rates of chemical change expressed?

   _____

   _____

2. Look at Figure 19.3 on page 534. In a typical reaction, as time passes, the

   amount of _____ decreases and the amount of

   _____ increases.

3. What does collision theory say about atoms, ions, or molecules reacting to form products when they collide?

   _____

   _____

   _____

4. Look at the figures below. One shows a collision that results in the formation of product. Label it *effective collision*. Label the other collision *ineffective collision*.

   _____   _____

5. Is the following sentence true or false? Particles lacking the necessary kinetic

   energy to react bounce apart unchanged when they collide. _____

6. Look at Figure 19.5 on page 535. Which arrangement of atoms contains the least amount of energy?

   a. reactants

   b. activated complex

   c. products

CHAPTER 19, Reaction Rates and Equilibrium *(continued)*

7. Circle the letter of the term that completes the sentence correctly. The minimum amount of energy that particles must have in order to react is called the _____ .

   a. kinetic energy   **c.** potential energy

   b. activation energy   **d.** collision energy

8. An activated complex is the arrangement of atoms at the _____ of the activation-energy barrier.

9. Circle the letter of the term that best describes the lifetime of an activated complex.

   a. 10^{-15} s   **b.** 10^{13} s   **c.** 10^{-13} s   **d.** 10^{-1} s

10. Why is an activated complex sometimes called the transition state?

   _____

   _____

▶ Factors Affecting Reaction Rates *(pages 536–538)*

11. Changes in the rate of chemical reactions depend on conditions such as

   _____ .

12. The main effect of increasing the temperature of a chemical reaction is to

   _____ the number of particles that have enough kinetic energy

   to react when they collide.

13. What happens when you put more reacting particles into a fixed volume?

   _____

   _____

14. Is the following sentence true or false? The smaller the particle size, the larger

   the surface area of a given mass of particles. _____

15. What are some ways to increase the surface area of solid reactants?

   _____

16. A _____ is a substance that increases the rate of a reaction

   without being used up itself during the reaction.

17. What does a catalyst do? _____

   _____

   _____

The graph below shows the reaction rate of the same reaction with and without a catalyst. Use it to help you answer Questions 18 and 19.

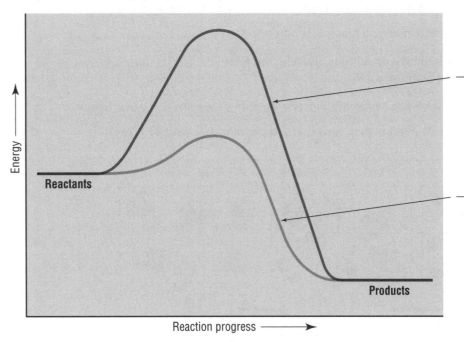

18. Label each curve as *with catalyst* or *without catalyst*.

19. What does the graph show about the effect of a catalyst on the rate of a

reaction? _____

_____

20. In a chemical equation, how do you show that catalysts are not consumed or

chemically altered during a reaction? _____

_____

21. A(n) _____ is a substance that interferes with the action of a catalyst.

SECTION 19.2 REVERSIBLE REACTIONS AND EQUILIBRIUM
(pages 539–548)

This section shows you how to predict changes in the equilibrium position due to changes in concentration, temperature, and pressure. It teaches you how to write the equilibrium-constant expression for a reaction and calculate its value from experimental data.

▶ **Reversible Reactions** (pages 539–541)

1. What happens in reversible reactions? _____

_____

CHAPTER 19, Reaction Rates and Equilibrium *(continued)*

2. Is the following sentence true or false? Chemical equilibrium is a state in which the forward and reverse reactions take place at different rates. _____

3. The equilibrium position of a reaction is given by the relative _____ of the system's components at equilibrium.

4. Fill in the missing labels on the diagram below with either the words *at equilibrium* or *not at equilibrium*. At equilibrium, how many types of molecules are present in the mixture? _____

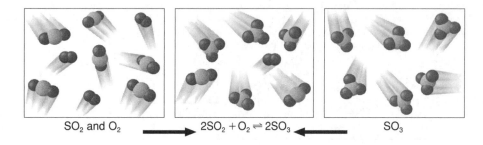

SO_2 and O_2 $2SO_2 + O_2 \rightleftharpoons 2SO_3$ SO_3

_____   _____   _____

5. Use Figure 19.10 on page 540 to answer these questions.

   a. Which graph, *a* or *b*, shows an initial concentration of 100% SO_3 and no SO_2? _____

   b. Compare the initial concentrations of the substances shown in the other graph.

   _____

   c. What is the favored substance at equilibrium? How can you tell?

   _____

▶ **Factors Affecting Equilibrium: Le Châtelier's Principle** (pages 541–544)

6. What is Le Châtelier's principle? _____

_____

7. Circle the letters of the terms that complete the sentence correctly. Stresses that upset the equilibrium of a chemical system include changes in _____ .

   a. concentration   c. pressure

   b. the amount of catalyst   d. temperature

8. When you add a product to a reversible chemical reaction, the reaction is always pushed in the direction of _____ . When you remove a product, the reaction is pulled in the direction of _____ .

9. Is the following sentence true or false? Increasing the temperature of a chemical reaction causes the equilibrium position of a reaction to shift in the direction that absorbs heat. _____

10. How does increasing pressure affect a chemical system? _____

_____

_____

11. Decreasing the pressure on the system shown in Figure 19.13 results in a shift of equilibrium to favor _____ .

▶ Equilibrium Constants (pages 545–548)

12. The equilibrium constant (K_{eq}) is the ratio of _____ concentrations to _____ concentrations at equilibrium, with each concentration raised to a power equal to the number of _____ of that substance in the balanced chemical equation.

13. What are the exponents in the equilibrium-constant expression?

_____

14. What do the square brackets indicate in the equilibrium-constant expression?

_____

_____

15. Is the following sentence true or false? The value of K_{eq} for a reaction depends on the temperature. _____

16. A value of K_{eq} greater than 1 means that _____ are favored over _____ . A value of K_{eq} less than 1 means that _____ are favored over _____ .

SECTION 19.3 DETERMINING WHETHER A REACTION WILL OCCUR
(pages 549–555)

This section defines entropy and free energy, and characterizes reactions as spontaneous or non-spontaneous. It also describes how heat change and entropy change determine the spontaneity of a reaction.

▶ Free Energy and Spontaneous Reactions (pages 549–551)

1. Free energy is energy that is available to do _____ .

2. Is the following sentence true or false? All processes can be made 100% efficient. _____

CHAPTER 19, Reaction Rates and Equilibrium *(continued)*

3. Make a concept map about balanced chemical reactions.

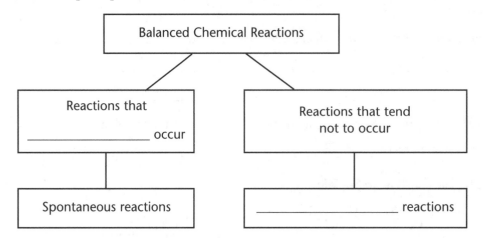

4. Spontaneous reactions are reactions that occur naturally and that favor the

formation of _____ at the specified conditions.

5. Describe four spontaneous reactions mentioned in this section.

   a. _____

   b. _____

   c. _____

   d. _____

6. What are nonspontaneous reactions?

   _____

   _____

7. Is the following sentence true or false? Some reactions that are non-

   spontaneous at one set of conditions may be spontaneous at other

   conditions. _____

▶ **Entropy** (pages 551–553)

8. Some factor other than _____ change must help determine

   whether a physical or chemical process is spontaneous.

9. What is entropy? _____

10. The law of disorder states that processes move in the direction of

    _____ disorder or randomness.

11. Is the following sentence true or false? Entropy decreases when a substance is

    divided into parts. _____

© Prentice-Hall, Inc.

12. Number the diagrams below from 1 to 3 to show the increasing entropy of the system. Diagram 1 should show the least amount of entropy.

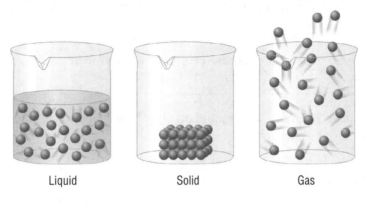

Liquid	Solid	Gas
_____	_____	_____

13. Does entropy tend to increase or decrease in chemical reactions in which the total number of product molecules is greater than the total number of reactant molecules? _____

14. Entropy tends to _____ when temperature increases.

▶ Heat, Entropy, and Free Energy (pages 554–555)

15. What determines whether a reaction is spontaneous?

_____

_____

16. Why is an exothermic reaction accompanied by an increase in entropy considered a spontaneous reaction? _____

17. Is the following sentence true or false? A nonspontaneous reaction, one in which the products are not favored, has heat changes, entropy changes, or both working against it. _____

SECTION 19.4 CALCULATING ENTROPY AND FREE ENERGY (pages 558–565)

This section teaches you how to calculate the standard entropy changes and the free-energy changes that accompany chemical and physical processes.

▶ Entropy Calculations (pages 558–561)

1. What is the symbol for entropy and what are the units? _____

2. The standard entropy of a liquid or solid substance at 25 °C is designated as _____ .

3. What is the pressure at S^0 for gaseous substances? _____

CHAPTER 19, Reaction Rates and Equilibrium (continued)

4. Is the following sentence true or false? The theoretical entropy of a perfect crystal at 0 K is zero. _____

5. What is the equation used to calculate standard entropy change (ΔS^0)?

   _____

6. Look at Table 19.2 on page 558. What is the standard entropy of calcium carbonate ($CaCO_3$)? _____

▶ Free-Energy Calculations (pages 561–565)

7. The Gibbs free-energy change (ΔG) is the maximum amount of energy that can be coupled to another process to do useful _____ .

8. What is the equation used to calculate the Gibbs free-energy change?

   _____

   _____

9. The numerical value of ΔG is _____ in spontaneous processes because the system loses free energy; the numerical value of ΔG is _____ in nonspontaneous processes because the system requires that work be expended to make them go forward at the specified conditions.

10. What is the equation used to calculate the standard free-energy change (ΔG^0) of a chemical reaction?_____

    _____

11. How do you calculate the standard free-energy change (ΔG^0) of a chemical reaction when ΔH^0 and ΔS^0 are unknown?_____

    _____

    _____

📖 Reading Skill Practice

Writing a summary can help you remember the information you have read. When you write a summary, include only the most important points. Write a summary of the information under the heading *Free Energy Calculations,* pages 561–563. Your summary should be shorter than the text on which it is based. Do your work on a separate sheet of paper.

SECTION 19.5 THE PROGRESS OF CHEMICAL REACTIONS
(pages 566–569)

This section describes how to use experimental rate data to deduce the rate laws for simple chemical reactions. It also shows how to analyze the mechanism for a reaction from an energy diagram.

▶ Rate Laws (pages 566–568)

1. What is a one-step reaction? _____

_____

2. Is the following sentence true or false? A rate law is an expression relating the

rate of a reaction to the concentration of products. _____

3. What is a specific rate constant (k) for a reaction? _____

_____

4. The _____ of a reaction is the power to which the concentration of a reactant must be raised to give the experimentally observed relationship between concentration and rate.

5. In a first-order reaction, the reaction rate is directly proportional to the concentration of _____ .

   a. two or more reactants

   b. both reactants and products

   c. only one reactant

6. How do you determine the actual kinetic order of a reaction?

_____

▶ Reaction Mechanisms (pages 568–569)

7. What is a reaction progress curve? _____

_____

8. A(n) _____ reaction is one in which reactants are converted to products in a single step.

9. Is the following sentence true or false? A reaction mechanism includes some of

the elementary reactions of a complex reaction. _____

10. What is an intermediate product of a reaction?

_____

11. Look at Figure 19.23 on page 569. What is one difference between this graph and the chemical equation for this reaction?

_____

MathWise

GUIDED PRACTICE PROBLEM 10 (page 546)

10. Suppose the following system reaches equilibrium at a high temperature.

$$N_2(g) + O_2(g) \rightleftharpoons 2NO(g)$$

An analysis of the equilibrium mixture in a 1-L flask gives the following results: nitrogen, 0.50 mol; oxygen, 0.50 mol; nitrogen monoxide, 0.020 mol. Calculate K_{eq} for the reaction.

Step 1. List the known values and the unknowns.

Known	Unknown
$[N_2]$ = _____	K_{eq} = ?
$[O_2]$ = _____	
$[NO]$ = 0.020 mol/L	

Step 2. Write the K_{eq} for the reaction. It should have three variables.

K_{eq} = _____

Step 3. Substitute the known values in the expression.

$$K_{eq} = \frac{(\boxed{} \text{ mol/L})^2}{\boxed{} \text{ mol/L} \times \boxed{} \text{ mol/L}}$$

Step 4. Solve. Write your answer in scientific notation.

$K_{eq} = 0.0016 = \boxed{}$

EXTRA PRACTICE (similar to Practice Problem 13, page 548)

13. Write the expression for the equilibrium constant for the reaction at the right.

$$4HCl(g) + O_2(g) \rightleftharpoons 2Cl_2(g) + 2H_2O(g)$$

GUIDED PRACTICE PROBLEM 26 (page 561)

26. Based on the data in Table 19.2, calculate ΔS^0 for converting the monoclinic form of sulfur to the rhombic form.

Step 1. Write the balanced equation.

S(s, _____ ⟶

S(s, _____)

Step 2. Find the S^0 values of the products and reactants.

S^0 for S (monoclinic) = _____ J/K·mol

S^0 for S (rhombic) = _____ J/K·mol

Step 3. Substitute into the formula $\Delta S^0 = S^0(\text{products}) - S^0(\text{reactants})$.

ΔS^0 = _____ J/K·mol − _____ J/K·mol

= _____ J/K·mol

20 ACIDS AND BASES

SECTION 20.1 DESCRIBING ACIDS AND BASES (pages 577–579)

This section lists the properties of acids and bases. It also explains how to name an acid or base when given the formula.

▶ Properties of Acids and Bases (pages 577–578)

1. Circle the letters of all the terms that complete the sentence correctly. The properties of acids include _____ .

   a. reacting with metals to produce oxygen

   b. giving foods a sour taste

   c. forming solutions that conduct electricity

   d. causing indicators to change color

2. Is the following sentence true or false? Acids react with compounds containing hydroxide ions to form water and a salt. _____

3. Bases are compounds that react with acids to form _____ and a(n) _____ .

4. Circle the letters of all the terms that complete the sentence correctly. The properties of bases include _____ .

   a. tasting bitter

   b. feeling slippery

   c. changing the color of an indicator

   d. always acting as a strong electrolyte

▶ Names and Formulas of Acids and Bases (pages 578–579)

5. What is an acid?

   _____

6. When the name of an anion in an acid ends in *-ide*, the acid name begins with the prefix _____ .

7. Give the general form of the chemical formula of an acid and tell what the letters in the formula stand for. _____

   _____

© Prentice-Hall, Inc.

CHAPTER 20, Acids and Bases *(continued)*

8. Look at Table 20.1 on page 578. Use it to help you complete this table of anions and the acids they can form.

Naming Acids	
Formula of Anion	Name of Acid
F^-	
SO_3^{2-}	
SO_4^{2-}	

9. Is the following sentence true or false? The rules for naming acids cannot

be used in reverse to write the formulas of acids from their names. _____

10. A base is a compound that produces _____ ions when dissolved in water.

11. How do you write the formula for bases?

_____

SECTION 20.2 HYDROGEN IONS AND ACIDITY (pages 580–592)

This section classifies solutions as neutral, acidic, or basic, given the hydrogen-ion or hydroxide-ion concentration. It explains how to convert hydrogen-ion concentrations into pH values and hydroxide-ion concentrations into pOH values.

▶ Hydrogen Ions from Water (pages 580–582)

1. What does a water molecule that loses a hydrogen ion become?

_____

2. What does a water molecule that gains a hydrogen ion become?

_____

3. The reaction in which two water molecules produce ions is called the

_____ of water.

4. In water or aqueous solution, _____ are always joined to

_____ as hydronium ions (H_3O^+).

5. Is the following sentence true or false? Any aqueous solution in which [H^+] and

[OH^-] are equal is described as a neutral solution. _____

© Prentice-Hall, Inc.

6. What is the ion-product constant for water (K_w)? Give the definition, the expression, and the value. _____

_____

_____

7. A(n) _____ solution is one in which [H^+] is greater than [OH^-].

A(n) _____ solution is one in which [H^+] is less than [OH^-].

8. Match the type of solution with its hydrogen-ion concentration.

_____ acidic   **a.** less than $1.0 \times 10^{-7} M$

_____ neutral   **b.** greater than $1.0 \times 10^{-7} M$

_____ basic   **c.** $1.0 \times 10^{-7} M$

▶ The pH Concept (pages 582–587)

9. The _____ of a solution is the negative logarithm of the hydrogen-ion concentration.

10. Match the type of solution with its pH.

_____ acidic   **a.** pH > 7.0

_____ neutral   **b.** pH = 7.0

_____ basic   **c.** pH < 7.0

11. Look at Table 20.2 on page 584. What is the approximate [H^+], the [OH^-], and the pH of washing soda? _____

12. The pOH of a solution is the negative logarithm of the _____ concentration.

13. What is the pOH of a neutral solution? _____

14. If you are making pH calculations, how should you express the hydrogen-ion concentration? _____

15. Look at the pH scale below. Label where you would find acids, bases, and neutral solutions.

pH

```
0   1   2   3   4   5   6   7   8   9   10  11  12  13  14
|   |   |   |   |   |   |   |   |   |   |   |   |   |   |
```

```
10⁰ 10⁻¹ 10⁻² 10⁻³ 10⁻⁴ 10⁻⁵ 10⁻⁶ 10⁻⁷ 10⁻⁸ 10⁻⁹ 10⁻¹⁰ 10⁻¹¹ 10⁻¹² 10⁻¹³ 10⁻¹⁴
```

CHAPTER 20, Acids and Bases *(continued)*

▶ Calculating pH Values (pages 587–589)

16. Is the following sentence true or false? Most pH values are whole numbers.

_____

17. If [H⁺] is written in scientific notation but its coefficient is not 1, what do you need to calculate pH? _____

_____

18. Is the following sentence true or false? You can calculate the hydrogen-ion concentration of a solution if you know the pH. _____

▶ Measuring pH (pages 589–592)

19. When do you use indicators and when do you use a pH meter to measure pH?

_____

_____

20. Why is an indicator a valuable tool for measuring pH?

_____

_____

21. Why do you need many different indicators to span the entire pH spectrum?

_____

_____

22. Look at the figure below. Fill in the missing pH color change ranges for the indicators.

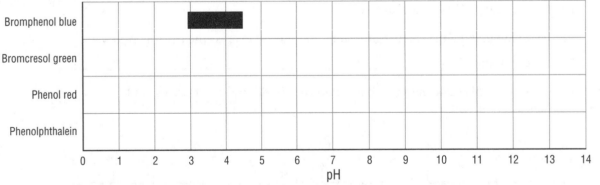

23. A pH meter uses a combination electrode connected to a millivoltmeter. What two electrodes make up this combination electrode?

_____

© Prentice-Hall, Inc.

24. List three characteristics that limit the usefulness of indicators.

a. _____

b. _____

c. _____

25. Complete the flow chart with the steps you would use to measure the pH of a solution with a pH meter.

```
┌─────────────────────────────────────────────────────────────┐
│                                                             │
│   First, _____ the meter by immersing its   │
│                                                             │
│   _____ in a solution of a known pH.        │
│                                                             │
└─────────────────────────────────────────────────────────────┘
                              │
                              ▼
┌─────────────────────────────────────────────────────────────┐
│                                                             │
│   Adjust the readout of the _____ to this known pH. │
│                                                             │
└─────────────────────────────────────────────────────────────┘
                              │
                              ▼
┌─────────────────────────────────────────────────────────────┐
│                                                             │
│   Then, rinse the electrodes with _____ .   │
│                                                             │
└─────────────────────────────────────────────────────────────┘
                              │
                              ▼
┌─────────────────────────────────────────────────────────────┐
│                                                             │
│   Finally, dip the electrodes into the solution of unknown _____ . │
│                                                             │
└─────────────────────────────────────────────────────────────┘
```

26. Is the following sentence true or false? Measurements of pH obtained with a pH meter are typically accurate to within 0.001 pH unit of the true pH.

_____

SECTION 20.3 ACID-BASE THEORIES (pages 594–599)

This section compares and contrasts acids and bases as defined by the theories of Arrhenius, Brønsted-Lowry, and Lewis. It also identifies conjugate acid-base pairs in acid-base reactions.

▶ Arrhenius Acids and Bases (pages 594–596)

1. Match the number of ionizable hydrogens with the type of acid.

_____ one   **a.** diprotic

_____ two   **b.** triprotic

_____ three   **c.** monoprotic

© Prentice-Hall, Inc.

CHAPTER 20, Acids and Bases *(continued)*

2. Is the following sentence true or false? Only the hydrogens in weak polar bonds are ionizable. _____

3. Hydrogen is joined to a very _____ element in a very polar bond.

4. Alkali metals react with water to produce _____ solutions.

5. How do concentrated basic solutions differ from other basic solutions?

_____

▶ Brønsted-Lowry Acids and Bases (pages 596–598)

6. How does the Brønsted-Lowry theory define acids and bases?

_____

_____

7. Is the following sentence true or false? Some of the acids and bases included in the Arrhenius theory are not acids and bases according to the Brønsted-Lowry theory. _____

8. Is the following sentence true or false? A conjugate acid is the particle formed when a base gains a hydrogen ion. _____

9. A conjugate _____ is the particle that remains when an acid has donated a hydrogen ion.

10. What is a conjugate acid-base pair? _____

_____

11. A substance that can act as both an acid and a base is said to be

_____ .

12. In a reaction with HCl, is water an acid or a base?

_____

▶ Lewis Acids and Bases (pages 598–599)

13. What is a Lewis acid? _____

_____

14. A Lewis base is a substance that can _____ a pair of electrons to form a covalent bond.

15. Is the following sentence true or false? All the acids and bases included in the Brønsted-Lowry theory are also acids and bases according to the Lewis theory.

_____

16. Complete this table of acid-base definitions.

Acid-Base Definitions		
Type	**Acid**	**Base**
Brønsted-Lowry		H^+ acceptor
	electron-pair acceptor	
	H^+ producer	

SECTION 20.4 STRENGTHS OF ACIDS AND BASES (pages 600–605)

This section defines strong acids and weak acids, and then explains how to calculate an acid dissociation constant. It describes how acids and bases are arranged by strength according to their dissociation constants (K_a) and (K_b).

▶ Strong and Weak Acids and Bases (pages 600–604)

1. What factor is used to classify acids as strong or weak?

_____

2. Strong acids are _____ ionized in aqueous solution; weak

acids ionize _____ in aqueous solution.

3. Look at Table 20.7 on page 600. Which acid is the weakest acid in the table? Which base is the weakest base?

_____

4. What do you use to write the equilibrium-constant expression?

_____

5. An acid dissociation constant (K_a) is the ratio of the concentration of the

_____ form of an acid to the concentration of the

_____ form.

6. What is another name for dissociation constants?

_____

7. Is the following sentence true or false? The stronger an acid is, the smaller its

K_a value. _____

CHAPTER 20, Acids and Bases *(continued)*

8. A diprotic acid has _____ dissociation constants.

9. Look at Table 20.8 on page 602. What is the second dissociation constant for the triprotic phosphoric acid? _____

10. Weak bases react with water to form the hydroxide ion and the

_____ of the base.

11. A base dissociation constant (K_b) is the ratio of the concentration of the

_____ times the concentration of the hydroxide

ion to the concentration of the _____ .

12. What does the magnitude of the base dissociation constant (K_b) indicate?

_____

_____

13. The words *concentrated* and *dilute* indicate how much acid or base is

_____ in solution.

14. Is the following sentence true or false? The words strong or weak refer to the extent of ionization or dissociation of an acid or base. _____

▶ Calculating Dissociation Constants *(pages 604–605)*

15. Is the following sentence true or false? You can calculate the acid dissociation constant (K_a) of a weak acid from experimental data. _____

16. To measure the equilibrium concentrations of all substances present at equilibrium for a weak acid, what two conditions must you know?

_____

_____

Reading Skill Practice

By looking carefully at photographs and drawings in textbooks, you can better understand what you have read. Look carefully at Figure 20.16 on page 601. What important idea does this drawing communicate? Do your work on a separate sheet of paper.

© Prentice-Hall, Inc.

MathWise

GUIDED PRACTICE PROBLEM 12b (page 588)

12b. Calculate the pH of this solution: $[H^+] = 8.3 \times 10^{-10}\, M$.

Step 1. Identify the known and unknown values.

Known

$[H^+] = \boxed{} \times 10^{-10}\, M$

Unknown

$pH = ?$

Step 2. Substitute values into the pH equation.

$pH = -\log [H^+]$

$= -\log (8.3 \times \boxed{})$

Step 3. The logarithm of a product equals the sum of the logs of its factors.

$= - (\log \boxed{} + \log \boxed{})$

Step 4. Evaluate log 8.3 by using a calculator or the log table in Appendix B. Evaluate $\log 10^{-10}$ by using the definition of logarithm.

$= -(0.919 + \boxed{})$

Step 5. Add and simplify. Write your answer with two significant figures to the right of the decimal point.

$= -(-9.081) = \boxed{}$

EXTRA PRACTICE PROBLEM (similar to Practice Problem 15, page 589)

15. Find the value of $[OH^-]$ for a solution with a pH of 8.00.

CHAPTER 20, Acids and Bases *(continued)*

GUIDED PRACTICE PROBLEM 26 (page 605)

26. For a solution of methanoic acid exactly 0.1 M, $[H^+] = -4.2 \times 10^{-3}M$. Calculate the K_a of methanoic acid.

Analyze

Step 1. What is known about the acid?

_____

_____

Step 2. What is the unknown? ____

_____

Step 3. What is the expression $K_a =$
for the K_a of methanoic acid?

_____

Solve

Step 4. What expression can you
write to find the equilibrium
concentration of HCOOH?   _____

_____

Step 5. Substitute values into the formula for K_a and solve.

_____

Analyze

Step 6. Look at Table 20.8 on page 602. Explain why your answer is reasonable.

_____

_____

21 NEUTRALIZATION

SECTION 21.1 NEUTRALIZATION REACTIONS (pages 613–624)

This section explains how acid–base titration is used to calculate the concentration of an acid or a base. It also explains the concept of equivalence in neutralization reactions.

▶ Acid–Base Reactions (pages 613–614)

1. What does the reaction of an acid with a base produce?

   _____

2. Salts are compounds consisting of a(n) _____ from an acid

   and a(n) _____ from a base.

3. In general, reactions in which an acid and a base react in an aqueous solution

   to produce a salt and water are called _____ reactions.

4. Look at Table 21.1 on page 614. Circle the letter of the salt that is used for plaster casts.

   a. calcium sulfate dihydrate   **c.** calcium sulfate hemihydrate

   b. copper sulfate pentahydrate   **d.** calcium chloride

▶ Titration (pages 615–618)

5. How can you determine the concentration of an acid or base in a solution?

   _____

6. Complete the flow chart below showing the steps of a neutralization reaction.

   ┌───┐
   │ A measured volume of an acid solution of _____   │
   │ concentration is added to a flask.   │
   └───┘
                              ↓
   ┌───┐
   │ Several drops of the _____ are added to the solution. │
   └───┘
                              ↓
   ┌───┐
   │ Measured volumes of a base of _____ concentration are │
   │ mixed into the acid until the indicator changes _____ . │
   └───┘

7. What is the solution of known concentration called?

   _____

© Prentice-Hall, Inc.

CHAPTER 21, Neutralization *(continued)*

8. The process of adding a known amount of solution of known concentration to

   determine the concentration of another solution is called _____ .

▶ Equivalents (pages 619–620)

9. One _____ is the amount of acid (or base) that will give one
   mole of hydrogen (or hydroxide) ions.

10. Is the following sentence true or false? In any neutralization reaction, the

    equivalents of acid must equal the equivalents of base. _____

11. What is a gram equivalent mass?

    _____

▶ Normality (pages 621–624)

12. The normality (*N*) of a solution is the concentration expressed as the number

    of _____ of solute in one _____ of solution.

13. In a titration, what do you call the point at which neutralization occurs?

    _____

📖 Reading Skill Practice

Writing a summary can help you remember the information you have read. When you write a summary, include only the most important points. Write a summary of the information under the heading *Normality*, pages 621–622. Your summary should be shorter than the text on which it is based. Do your work on a separate sheet of paper.

SECTION 21.2 SALTS IN SOLUTION (pages 626–637)

This section demonstrates with equations how buffers resist changes in pH. It also explains how to calculate the solubility product constant of a slightly soluble salt.

▶ Salt Hydrolysis (pages 626–627)

1. What is salt hydrolysis? _____

   _____

   _____

© Prentice-Hall, Inc.

2. Complete this table of the rules for hydrolysis of a salt.

Reactants		Products
_____ acid + _____ base		Neutral solution
Strong acid + Weak base		_____ solution
_____ acid + _____ base		Basic solution

▶ Buffers (pages 628–630)

3. What are buffers? _____

_____

4. A buffer is a solution of a _____ acid and one of its salts,

or a solution of a _____ base and one of its salts.

5. Is the following sentence true or false? The buffer capacity is the amount of

acid or base that can be added to a buffer solution before a significant change

in pH occurs. _____

▶ The Solubility Product Constant (pages 630–635)

6. What is the solubility product constant (K_{sp})?

_____

_____

7. Look at Table 21.3 on page 631. Which ionic compounds are exceptions to the
general insolubility of carbonates, phosphates, and sulfites?

_____

8. Look at Table 21.4 on page 632. Which salt is more soluble in water, silver

bromide (AgBr) or silver chromate (Ag_2CrO_4)? _____

▶ The Common Ion Effect (pages 635–637)

9. A common ion is an ion that is common to both _____ in
a solution.

10. Is the following sentence true or false? The raising of the solubility of a

substance by the addition of a common ion is called the common ion

effect. _____

11. A solubility product can be used to predict whether a _____
will form when solutions are mixed.

MathWise

GUIDED PRACTICE PROBLEM 3 (page 618)

3. How many milliliters of 0.45M hydrochloric acid must be added to 25.0 mL of 1.00M potassium hydroxide to make a neutral solution?

Step 1. List the known and unknown values.

Known
0.45M solution of _____

_____ solution of KOH

_____ mL of KOH solution

Unknown
HCl = ? mL

Step 2. Write the equation for the neutralization of KOH by HCl. Then write the mole ratio of HCl and KOH.

$HCl + KOH \rightarrow$ _____ $+ H_2O$

$$\text{Mole ratio} = \frac{\boxed{} \text{ mol HCl}}{\boxed{} \text{ mol KOH}}$$

Step 3. Write the sequence of conversions needed.

mL KOH $\rightarrow$ _____ $\rightarrow$ _____
$\rightarrow$ mL HCl

Step 4. Write a product of conversion factors.

25.0 mL KOH $\times \dfrac{1\,\boxed{}}{1000 \text{ mL KOH}} \times \dfrac{\boxed{} \text{ mol HCl}}{\boxed{} \text{ mol KOH}} \times \dfrac{1000\,\boxed{} \text{ HCl}}{0.45\,\boxed{}}$

Step 5. Simplify the expression.

$\boxed{}$ mL HCl = $\boxed{}$ HCl

$\boxed{}$

EXTRA PRACTICE PROBLEM (similar to Practice Problem 10, page 621)

10. What is the normality of 98 g of sulfuric acid in 500 mL of solution?

EXTRA PRACTICE PROBLEM (similar to Practice Problem 12, page 623)

12. How would you prepare 1 liter of 0.20N sulfuric acid from a stock solution of 4.0N sulfuric acid?

GUIDED PRACTICE PROBLEM 15 (page 624)

15. How many milliliters of 0.850N hydrochloric acid do you need to neutralize 25.0 L of 0.480N sodium hydroxide?

Analyze

Step 1. What is the known information?

_____

Step 2. What is the unknown value?

_____

Step 3. What formula relates the normalities and volumes of neutralizing amounts of acids and bases?

_____

Solve

Step 4. Substitute values into the equation and solve.

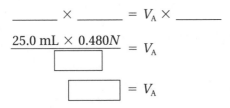

$$\text{_____} \times \text{_____} = V_A \times \text{_____}$$

$$\frac{25.0\ \text{mL} \times 0.480N}{\boxed{}} = V_A$$

$$\boxed{} = V_A$$

Analyze

Step 5. How do you know that the amount is reasonable?

_____

_____

_____

_____

Step 6. How many significant figures should the answer have?

_____

_____

_____

_____

CHAPTER 21, Neutralization *(continued)*

EXTRA PRACTICE PROBLEM *(similar to Practice Problem 16, page 624)*

16. How many milliliters of 2.00*N* sodium hydroxide are needed to neutralize 50.0 mL of 0.640*N* sulfuric acid?

GUIDED PRACTICE PROBLEM 27 *(page 635)*

27. The K_{sp} of silver sulfide (Ag_2S) is 8×10^{-51}. What is the silver-ion concentration of a saturated solution of silver sulfide? What is the sulfide-ion concentration of the same solution?

Step 1. List the knowns and unknowns.

Known

$K_{sp} = 8 \times$ ____

$Ag_2S \rightleftharpoons 2Ag^+ + S^{2-}$

Unknown

[   ] = 2*x*   [   ] = *x*

Step 2. Write the expression for K_{sp}.　$K_{sp} = (2x)^2\,(x) = \boxed{}$

Step 3. Substitute values and solve for x^3.

$8 \times \boxed{} = 4x^3$

$2 \times 10^{-51} = \boxed{}$

Step 4. Use a calculator or table of cube roots to find the cube root of 2. Divide $^-$51 by 3 to find the cube root of 10^{-51}.

$1.26 \times \boxed{} = x$

Step 5. Write the answers with the correct number of significant figures.

The sulfide ion concentration is

$\boxed{}$.

The silver ion concentration is

$\boxed{}$.

22 OXIDATION-REDUCTION REACTIONS

SECTION 22.1 THE MEANING OF OXIDATION AND REDUCTION (pages 645–653)

This section explains oxidation and reduction in terms of the loss or gain of electrons, and describes the characteristics of a redox reaction. It also explains how to identify oxidizing and reducing agents.

▶ Oxygen in Redox Reactions (pages 645–647)

1. What was the original meaning of the term *oxidation?* _____

_____

2. Circle the letter of each sentence that is true about oxidation.

   a. Gasoline, wood, coal, and natural gas (methane) can all burn in air, producing oxides of carbon.

   b. All oxidation processes involve burning.

   c. Bleaching is an example of oxidation.

   d. Rusting is an example of oxidation.

3. Look at Figure 22.2 and Figure 22.3 on page 646. Describe what is happening in each chemical reaction.

   a. $CH_4(g) + 2O_2(g) \longrightarrow CO_2(g) + 2H_2O(g)$ _____

   _____

   _____

   b. $4Fe(s) + 3O_2(g) \longrightarrow 2Fe_2O_3(s)$ _____

   _____

4. What is the name of the process that is the opposite of oxidation?

   _____

5. Circle the letter of each sentence that is true about oxidation and reduction.

   a. Oxidation never occurs without reduction and reduction never occurs without oxidation.

   b. You need to add heat in order to reduce iron ore to produce metallic iron.

   c. When iron oxide is reduced to metallic iron, it gains oxygen.

   d. Oxidation–reduction reactions are also known as redox reactions.

6. What substance is heated along with iron ore in order to reduce the metal

   oxide to metallic iron? _____

CHAPTER 22, Oxidation-Reduction Reactions *(continued)*

7. Look at Figure 22.4 on page 647. What do the iron artifacts tell you about what chemistry early Iron Age people knew 2500 years ago? _____

_____

8. Look at the chemical equation for the reduction of iron ore on page 647. When iron ore is reduced to metallic iron, what oxidation reaction occurs at the same time? _____

▶ Electron Transfer in Redox Reactions (pages 647–651)

9. Is the following sentence true or false? The concepts of oxidation and reduction have been extended to include many reactions that do not even involve oxygen. _____

10. What is understood about electrons in redox reactions?

_____

11. In the table below, fill in either "Gain" or "Loss" to correctly describe what happens to electrons or oxygen during oxidation or reduction.

	Oxidation	**Reduction**
Electrons		
Oxygen		

12. Look at Figure 22.5 on page 648. Circle the letter of each sentence that is true about the reaction of magnesium and sulfur.

a. When magnesium and sulfur are heated together, they undergo a redox reaction to form magnesium sulfide.

b. Electrons are transferred from the metal atoms to the nonmetal atoms in this reaction.

c. When magnesium atoms lose electrons and sulfur atoms gain electrons, the atoms become less stable.

d. Magnesium is the oxidizing agent and sulfur is the reducing agent in this reaction.

13. Is the following sentence true or false? In any redox reaction, complete electron transfer must occur. _____

14. Is the following sentence true or false? A redox reaction may produce covalent compounds. _____

© Prentice-Hall, Inc.

15. Draw arrows showing the shift of bonding electrons during formation of a water molecule. Then complete the table listing the characteristics of this reaction.

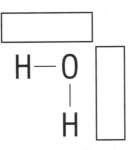

Formation of Water by Reaction of Hydrogen and Oxygen	
Chemical equation	
Shift of bonding electrons	
Reduced element	
Oxidized element	
Reducing agent	
Oxidizing agent	
Is heat released or absorbed?	

16. For each process described below, label it *O* if it is an oxidation or *R* if it is a reduction.

_____ **a.** Addition of oxygen to carbon or carbon compounds

_____ **b.** Removal of a metal from its ore

_____ **c.** Complete gain of electrons in an ionic reaction

_____ **d.** Shift of electrons away from an atom in a covalent bond

_____ **e.** Gain of hydrogen by a covalent compound

▶ Corrosion (pages 651–653)

17. Circle the letter of each sentence that is true about corrosion.

a. Preventing and repairing damage from corrosion of metals requires billions of dollars every year.

b. Iron corrodes by being oxidized to ions of iron by oxygen.

c. Water in the environment slows down the rate of corrosion.

d. The presence of salts and acids increases the rate of corrosion by producing conducting solutions that make the transfer of electrons easier.

CHAPTER 22, Oxidation-Reduction Reactions *(continued)*

18. Why are gold and platinum called noble metals? _____

_____

19. Look at Figure 22.7 on page 651. Why is corrosion desirable in the situation

    shown? _____

_____

20. Look at Figure 22.8 on page 652. Complete the sketch below to show how
    oxides form on the surface of each metal. Explain how differences between the
    oxides affect further corrosion of the metals.

_____

_____

_____

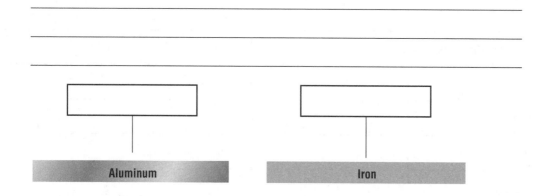

Aluminum   Iron

SECTION 22.2   OXIDATION NUMBERS (pages 654–659)

This section explains how to determine the oxidation number of an atom of any element in a pure substance and defines oxidation and reduction in terms of a change in oxidation number.

▶ Assigning Oxidation Numbers (pages 654–656)

1. Is the following sentence true or false? As a general rule, a bonded atom's

   oxidation number is the charge that it would have if the electrons in the bond

   were assigned to the more electronegative element. _____

2. For each binary ionic compound listed in the table, write the symbols for both
   ions, their ionic charges, and their oxidation numbers.

Compound	Ions	Ionic Charges	Oxidation Numbers
NaCl			
CaF$_2$			

3. Is the following sentence true or false? Even though water is a molecular compound, you can still obtain oxidation numbers for the bonded elements by pretending that the electrons contributed by the hydrogen atoms are completely transferred to oxygen. _____

4. Write the oxidation number, or the sum of the oxidation numbers, for the given atoms, ions, or compounds.

_____ a. Cu(II) ion

_____ b. Hydrogen in water

_____ c. Hydrogen in sodium hydride (NaH)

_____ d. Potassium sulfate (K_2SO_4)

▶ Oxidation-Number Changes in Chemical Reactions (pages 657–659)

5. Label each change *O* if it describes oxidation or *R* if it describes reduction.

_____ a. Decrease in the oxidation number of an element

_____ b. Increase in the oxidation number of an element

SECTION 22.3 BALANCING REDOX EQUATIONS (pages 660–669)

This section explains how to use the oxidation-number-change and half-reaction methods to balance redox equations.

▶ Identifying Redox Reactions (pages 660–663)

1. Name two kinds of reactions that are not redox reactions.

_____

2. Look at Figure 22.15 on page 660. Write the oxidation numbers of all the elements in the reactants and products. Then answer the questions about the reaction.

	Reactants		**Products**	
	Zinc	Hydrochloric acid	Zinc chloride	Hydrogen
Oxidation numbers	_____	_____	_____	_____
Chemical equation	Zn(*s*) +	HCl(*aq*) $\longrightarrow$	ZnCl$_2$(*aq*) +	H$_2$(*g*)

a. Is this a redox reaction? _____

b. Which element is oxidized? How do you know?

_____

c. Which element is reduced? How do you know?

_____

© Prentice-Hall, Inc.

CHAPTER 22, Oxidation-Reduction Reactions *(continued)*

3. When a solution changes color during a reaction, what can you conclude about the reaction that has taken place?

_____

▶ Using Oxidation-Number Changes (pages 663–665)

4. Answer these questions to help you balance the following equation using the oxidation-number-change method.

$$H_2(g) + O_2(g) \longrightarrow H_2O(l) \text{ (unbalanced)}$$

a. What are the oxidation numbers for each atom in the equation?

b. Which element is oxidized in this reaction? Which is reduced?

_____

c. Use your answers to question *a* above to balance the equation. Write the coefficients needed to make the total change in oxidation number equal to 0.

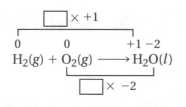

d. What is the final balanced equation? _____

▶ Using Half-Reactions (pages 665–669)

5. The equations for which reactions are balanced separately when using the

half-reaction method? _____

_____

6. For what kind of reaction is the half-reaction method particularly useful?

_____

📖 Reading Skill Practice

A flowchart can help you to remember the order in which events occur. On a separate sheet of paper, create a flowchart that describes the steps for the oxidation-number-change method. This process is explained on pages 663–664 of your textbook.

MathWise

GUIDED PRACTICE PROBLEM 9 (page 656)

9. Determine the oxidation number of each element in these substances.

a. S_2O_3 _____

Step 1. What is the oxidation number for oxygen? Use rule 3. _____

Step 2. What is the oxidation number for all of the oxygen atoms?

_____

Step 3. What is the oxidation number for all of the sulfur atoms? _____

_____

Step 4. What is the oxidation number for each sulfur atom? _____

_____

Step 5. How do you know your answers are correct?

_____

b. O_2 _____

Step 1. What type of substance is O_2? _____

Step 2. What is the oxidation number of
oxygen? Use rule 4. _____

c. $Al_2(SO_4)_3$ _____

Step 1. What is the charge of the polyatomic
sulfate ion? _____

Step 2. What is the oxidation number of
oxygen? Use rule 3. _____

Step 3. What is the oxidation number
of all of the oxygen atoms? _____

Step 4. What is the oxidation number
of the sulfur atom? _____

Step 5. What is the oxidation number
of the aluminum ion? _____

CHAPTER 22, Oxidation-Reduction Reactions *(continued)*

d. Na_2O_2 _____

Step 1. What is the oxidation number of
oxygen? Use rule 3. (Hint: This compound
is a peroxide.)

_____

Step 2. What is the oxidation
number of sodium?

_____

Step 3. How do you know your answer
is correct?

The oxidation number for both

oxygen atoms is _____ . The sum of

the oxidation numbers for all the

atoms must be _____ . Therefore,

the oxidation number for both

sodium atoms must equal _____ .

EXTRA PRACTICE (similar to Practice Problem 19, page 664)

19. Balance this redox equation using the oxidation-number-change method.

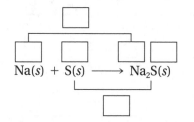

$$Na(s) + S(s) \longrightarrow Na_2S(s)$$

To make the oxidation numbers balance, you must multiply the oxidation number of

sodium by _____ . Add a coefficient of _____ in front of elemental sodium,

but not in front of sodium sulfate because the sodium in sodium sulfate has a

subscript of _____ . The balanced equation is _____ .

ⓐ ELECTROCHEMISTRY

SECTION 23.1 ELECTROCHEMICAL CELLS (pages 677–684)

This section describes how redox reactions interconvert electrical energy and chemical energy. It also explains the structure of a dry cell and identifies the substances that are oxidized and reduced.

▶ The Nature of Electrochemical Cells (pages 677–679)

1. What do the silver plating of tableware and the manufacture of aluminum have in common?

_____

Look at Figure 23.1 on page 677 and the related text to help you answer Questions 2–6.

2. In what form are the reactants when the reaction starts?

_____

3. What kind of reaction occurs? Is it spontaneous?

_____

4. Which substance is oxidized in the reaction? _____

5. Which substance is reduced? _____

6. Which atoms lose electrons and which ions gain electrons during the reaction?

_____

7. Look at Table 23.1 on page 678. What information in this table explains why the reaction in Figure 23.1 occurs spontaneously?

_____

_____

_____

_____

8. What happens when a copper strip is placed in a solution of zinc sulfate? Explain.

_____

_____

9. The flow of _____ from zinc to copper is an electric

_____ .

CHAPTER 23, Electrochemistry *(continued)*

10. Circle the letter of each sentence that is true about electrochemical cells.

   a. An electrochemical cell either produces an electric current or uses an electric current to produce a chemical change.

   b. Redox reactions occur in electrochemical cells.

   c. For an electrochemical cell to be a source of useful electrical energy, the electrons must pass through an external circuit.

   d. An electrochemical cell can convert chemical energy to electrical energy, but not electrical energy into chemical energy.

▶ Voltaic Cells (pages 679–681)

For Questions 11–15, match each description with the correct term by writing its letter in the blank.

_____ **11.** Any electrochemical cell used to convert chemical energy into electrical energy

_____ **12.** One part of a voltaic cell in which either reduction or oxidation occurs

_____ **13.** The electrode at which oxidation occurs

_____ **14.** A tube containing a strong electrolyte, which allows transport of ions between the half-cells

_____ **15.** The electrode at which reduction occurs

   a. cathode

   b. salt bridge

   c. voltaic cell

   d. half-cell

   e. anode

▶ Dry Cells (pages 681–682)

16. Look at Figure 23.4 on page 681. How is a common dry cell constructed?

_____

_____

_____

17. Why are alkaline cells better and longer lasting than common cells?

_____

_____

18. Which element is oxidized in a dry cell? Which element is reduced?

_____

▶ **Lead Storage Batteries** (pages 682–683)

19. What is a battery? _____

20. How many voltaic cells are connected inside a lead storage battery typically found in a car? About how many volts are produced by each cell and what is the total voltage of such a battery?

_____

_____

21. Look at Figure 23.5 on page 682. In the diagram below label the following parts of a lead storage battery: electrolyte, anode, and cathode. Also indicate where oxidation and reduction occur while the battery is discharging.

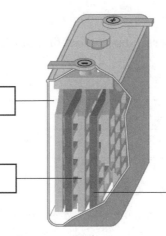

22. Are the following sentences true or false? As a lead storage battery discharges, lead sulfate builds up on the electrodes. Recharging the battery reverses this process. _____

▶ **Fuel Cells** (pages 683–684)

23. Name two advantages of fuel cells. _____

_____

📖 **Reading Skill Practice**

Outlining is a way to help you understand and remember what you have read. Write an outline for Section 23.1 *Electrochemical Cells*. Begin your outline by copying the headings in the textbook. Under each heading, write the main idea. Then list details that support, or back up, the main idea. Do your work on a separate sheet of paper.

CHAPTER 23, Electrochemistry *(continued)*

SECTION 23.2 HALF-CELLS AND CELL POTENTIALS (pages 685–691)

This section defines standard cell potential and standard reduction potential. It also explains how to use standard reduction potential to calculate standard cell potential.

▶ **Electrical Potential** (page 685)

1. What unit is usually used to measure electrical potential?

   _____

2. What is the equation for cell potential? _____

▶ **Standard Cell Potential** (pages 685–686)

3. What value have chemists assigned as the standard reduction potential of the

   hydrogen electrode? _____

4. Describe a standard hydrogen electrode. _____

   _____

   _____

▶ **Standard Reduction Potentials** (pages 686–688)

5. Use of a standard hydrogen electrode allows scientists to determine the

   _____ for many half-cells.

6. Look at Figure 23.9 on page 686. Which substance, zinc metal or hydrogen gas, has a greater potential to be oxidized? How can you tell?

   _____

   _____

7. In the diagram below use the value given for E^0_{cell} above the voltmeter and Table 23.2 to identify the chemical substances in the left half-cell. Use symbols to label the metal electrode and the ions in the half-cell. Also label the cathode and the anode.

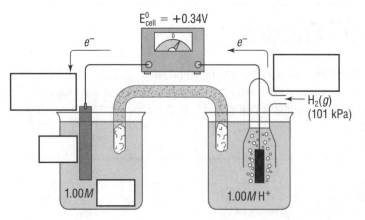

$E^0_{cell} = +0.34V$

e^- e^-

$H_2(g)$
(101 kPa)

1.00M 1.00M H$^+$

▶ Calculating Standard Cell Potentials (pages 689–691)

8. If the cell potential for a given redox reaction is _____ ,

then the reaction is _____ . If the cell potential is

_____ , then the reaction is _____ .

SECTION 23.3 ELECTROLYTIC CELLS (pages 692–697)

This section differentiates electrolytic cells from voltaic cells, and lists uses of electrolytic cells. It also identifies the products of the electrolysis of brine, molten sodium chloride, and water.

▶ Electrolysis of Water (pages 692–694)

1. An electrochemical cell used to cause a chemical change through the

application of electrical energy is called _____ .

2. For each sentence below, fill in *V* if it is true about voltaic cells, *E* if it is true about electrolytic cells, and *B* if it is true about both voltaic and electrolytic cells.

_____ **a.** Electrons are pushed by an outside power source.

_____ **b.** Reduction occurs at the cathode and oxidation occurs at the anode.

_____ **c.** The flow of electrons is the result of a spontaneous redox reaction.

_____ **d.** Electrons flow from the anode to the cathode.

▶ Electrolysis of Brine (pages 694–695)

3. Which three important industrial chemicals are produced through the electrolysis of brine?

_____

4. Why are the sodium ions not reduced to sodium metal during the electrolysis of brine?

_____

▶ Electrolysis of Molten Sodium Chloride (pages 695–696)

5. Which two important industrial chemicals are produced through the electrolysis of molten sodium chloride?

_____

▶ Electroplating and Related Processes (pages 696–697)

6. Deposition of a thin layer of metal on an object in an electrolytic cell is called

_____ .

7. The object to be plated is made the _____ in the cell.

© Prentice-Hall, Inc.

MathWise

GUIDED PRACTICE PROBLEM 8 (page 689)

8. A voltaic cell is constructed using the following half-reactions.

$Cu^{2+}(aq) + 2e^- \longrightarrow Cu(s)$ $E^0_{Cu^{2+}} = +0.34\,V$

$Al^{3+}(aq) + 3e^- \longrightarrow Al(s)$ $E^0_{Al^{3+}} = -1.66\,V$

Determine the cell reaction and calculate the standard cell potential.

Analyze

Step 1. What are the known values?

_____

Step 2. Which half-reaction is a reduction? An oxidation?

Reduction: _____

Oxidation: _____

Step 3. Write both half-reactions in the direction they actually occur.

_____

Step 4. What is the expression for the standard cell potential?

E^0_{cell} = _____

Solve

Step 5. Write the cell reaction by adding the half-reactions, making certain that the number of electrons lost equals the number of electrons gained. The electrons gained and lost will cancel out.

☐ $[Cu^{2+}(aq) + 2e^- \longrightarrow Cu(s)]$

☐ $[Al(s) \longrightarrow Al^{3+}(aq) + 3e^-]$

_____

☐

Step 6. Calculate the standard cell potential.

E^0_{cell} = _____

Evaluate

Step 7. How do you know that the cell reaction is correct?

_____

Step 8. When a reaction is spontaneous, will the standard cell potential be positive or negative?

_____

24 THE CHEMISTRY OF METALS AND NONMETALS

SECTION 24.1 THE *s*-BLOCK ELEMENTS: ACTIVE METALS (pages 705–710)

This section lists sources, properties, and uses for the alkali metals (Group 1A) and their compounds. It also describes the preparation and properties of the alkaline-earth metals (Group 2A) and gives uses for their compounds.

▶ The Alkali Metals (pages 705–706)

1. The alkali metals are in _____ on the periodic table.

2. Is the following sentence true or false? Alkali metal salts are very soluble in
   water. _____

3. How are alkali metals found in nature?

   _____

4. What happens when an alkali metal reacts with cold water?

   _____

   _____

5. Alkali metals are usually stored under _____ .

6. List five general characteristics of alkali metals.

   _____   _____

   _____   _____

   _____

7. Is the following sentence true or false? Potassium is the only alkali metal
   manufactured on a large scale. _____

8. Metallic sodium is generally produced by the _____ of
   molten sodium chloride.

▶ The Alkaline Earth Metals (pages 708–710)

9. The alkaline earth metals are the elements of _____ .

10. Is the following sentence true or false? Alkaline earth metal salts are more
    soluble in water than are the corresponding alkali metal salts.

    _____

11. What do the alkaline earth metals produce when they react with water?

    _____

© Prentice-Hall, Inc.

CHAPTER 24, The Chemistry of Metals and Nonmetals *(continued)*

12. Color and label the location of the alkaline earth metals in the figure below.

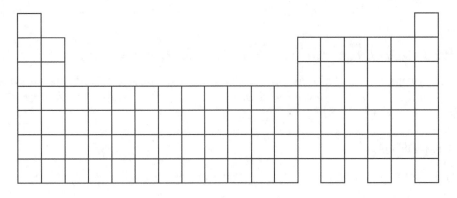

13. Although the alkaline earth metals are not found uncombined in nature, they are

_____ reactive than the alkali metals in Group 1A.

14. Which are the two most important alkaline earth metals?

_____

15. What is the common name for calcium oxide? _____

SECTION 24.2 THE *p*-BLOCK ELEMENTS: METALS AND NONMETALS
(pages 712–723)

This section describes properties and uses of the p-block metals and nonmetals. It also explains methods for obtaining specific p-block metals and nonmetals from their compounds and minerals.

▶ Aluminum and Group 3A (pages 712–713)

1. How does boron occur naturally?

_____

2. What is the chemical sodium tetraborate decahydrate ($Na_2B_4O_7 \cdot 10H_2O$)?

_____

3. Pure boron is black, lustrous, and extremely hard but brittle. It is also a

metalloid, or _____ .

4. The compound boron carbide is used to make machine tools because it is

almost as hard as _____ .

5. _____ is the most abundant metal in Earth's crust.

6. Name the metal elements in Group 3A.

_____   _____

_____   _____

© Prentice-Hall, Inc.

7. Complete the sentence with the letter of the correct term(s). Cut forms of corundum (impure aluminum oxide) with trace amounts of other elements are the gemstones _____ .

   a. diamond

   b. ruby

   c. emerald

   d. sapphire

   e. citrine

8. Look at Figure 24.9 on page 713. Aluminum is used in aircraft production

   because it is _____ , _____ , and resists

   _____ .

9. Is the following sentence true or false? The Group 3A elements, other than

   boron and aluminum, are quite rare. _____

▶ Carbon and Group 4A (page 714)

10. Which elements in Group 4A are two of the most important elements on Earth?

    _____

11. The three allotropes of carbon are _____ ,

    _____ , and _____ .

12. Which two elements in Group 4A are semiconductors?

    _____

13. Match the element with its use.

    _____ silicon   **a.** electrodes in storage batteries

    _____ tin   **b.** computer chips

    _____ lead   **c.** alloys such as bronze and solder

14. Why is lead no longer used in plumbing and in gasoline?

    _____

▶ Nitrogen and Group 5A (pages 715–717)

15. Which elements in Group 5A are nonmetals?

    _____

16. Is the following sentence true or false? Nitrogen can be used by the human

    body in its elemental form. _____

CHAPTER 24, The Chemistry of Metals and Nonmetals *(continued)*

17. Plants use fixed nitrogen compounds to synthesize _____ and other biologically important nitrogen-containing compounds.

18. The most important industrial uses of atmospheric nitrogen are in the

     manufacture of _____ and _____ .

19. Which Group 5A element other than nitrogen is essential to living

     organisms? _____

▶ Oxygen and Group 6A (pages 717–721)

20. Which elements in Group 6A are nonmetals? _____

21. _____ is Earth's most abundant element.

22. Circle the letter of locations where ozone (O_3) is produced.

    a. in silicate rocks   **c.** near high-voltage generators

    b. Earth's upper atmosphere   **d.** in liquified air

23. Where do you find sulfur in the elemental state? _____

    _____

24. Circle the letter of the number of sulfur atoms in each molecule of crystalline sulfur.

    a. 2   **b.** 4   **c.** 6   **d.** 8

25. Complete the flowchart for the production of sulfuric acid.

    $$SO_2(g) + \boxed{} \xrightarrow{V_2O_5} \boxed{} + H_2O \longrightarrow \boxed{}$$

▶ The Halogens (pages 721–723)

26. Color and label the location of the halogens in the figure below.

27. Is the following sentence true or false? The halogens exist in nature in the

     uncombined state. _____

28. Which elements in Group 7A are gases at room temperature?

     _____

29. Halide ions are abundant in _____ water and in

_____ formed by the evaporation of salt water.

30. Which halogen is the most chemically reactive of all the nonmetals?

_____

31. Describe two important uses for chlorine.

a. _____

b. _____

📖 Reading Skill Practice

By looking carefully at photographs and drawings in textbooks, you can better understand what you have read. Look carefully at Figure 24.13 on page 715. What important idea does this drawing communicate? Do your work on a separate sheet of paper.

SECTION 24.3   THE *d*- AND *f*-BLOCK ELEMENTS: TRANSITION AND INNER TRANSITION METALS (pages 724–731)

This section lists the properties of specific transition metals. It also describes the chemical diversity shown by the transition metals and inner transition metals.

▶ Overview (pages 724–726)

1. What are minerals used for the commercial production of metals called?

_____

2. _____ is the use of various procedures to separate metals from their ores.

3. Complete the list of basic steps used to separate metals from their ores.

a. _____ the ore

b. chemically _____ the ore to the metal

c. refining and _____ the metal

4. Is the following sentence true or false? As atomic number increases among the transition metals, there is an increase in the number of electrons in the second-to-highest energy level. _____

CHAPTER 24, The Chemistry of Metals and Nonmetals *(continued)*

5. Look at Table 24.4 on page 725. Match the transition metal with its use.

_____ cobalt   **a.** filaments for light bulbs

_____ tungsten   **b.** electrical wiring

_____ platinum   **c.** treatment of cancer

_____ copper   **d.** as a catalyst

▶ Titanium, Chromium, and Zinc (pages 726–727)

6. Match the element with its use(s).

_____ titanium   **a.** brass   **d.** in dry cell batteries

_____ zinc   **b.** sunscreen   **e.** stainless steel

_____ chromium   **c.** galvanized steel **f.** aircraft engines

7. What are the most common oxidation states of chromium?

_____

▶ Iron, Cobalt, and Nickel (pages 727–728)

8. List the metals iron, cobalt, and nickel in order from least to most magnetic.

_____

9. Complete the diagram by filling in the missing labels. This diagram shows iron being produced in a blast furnace. What is oxidized in this reaction?

_____

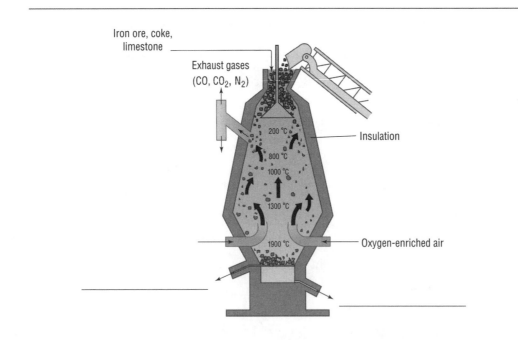

10. There are two types of steels. _____ steels contain no

_____ other than iron. _____ steels contain

other _____ in small amounts.

11. Monel metal is a strong, corrosion-resistant alloy of _____

and _____ .

▶ Copper, Silver, and Gold (pages 728-730)

12. Do copper, silver, and gold occur in the free state naturally or are they

combined with nonmetals? What is the collective name for these metals?

_____

13. Brass is an alloy of copper with _____ ; bronze is an alloy

of copper with _____ .

14. Is the following sentence true or false? Both gold and silver resist corrosion.

_____

15. What property of silver makes it useful as a coating for mirrors?

_____

16. Explain why gold alloys are used in jewelry.

_____

▶ Lanthanides and Actinides (page 731)

17. The lanthanides and actinides are called the _____
because their seven inner $4f$ and $5f$ orbitals, respectively, are being filled.

18. Why is it difficult to separate individual lanthanides from their ores?

_____

19. What are elements with atomic numbers greater than 92 called?

_____

SECTION 24.4 HYDROGEN AND NOBLE GASES (pages 732-735)

This section shows how hydrogen is unique among the elements. It explains why the noble gases, Group 0, are important even though they are extremely unreactive.

▶ Hydrogen—A Group by Itself (pages 732-733)

1. What is the most abundant hydrogen-containing compound on Earth?

_____

CHAPTER 24, The Chemistry of Metals and Nonmetals (continued)

2. Name the three naturally occurring isotopes of hydrogen.

_____

3. Where does hydrogen usually appear in the periodic table?

_____

4. Is the following sentence true or false? Hydrogen loses its single electron with great difficulty. _____

5. What is the major industrial use of hydrogen?

_____

6. The name of the process that converts vegetable oils into solid fats is

_____ .

7. What is the name of the process that is used to prepare hydrogen commercially from water? _____

▶ The Noble Gases (page 734)

8. Is the following sentence true or false? The Group 0 gases tend to exist as separate atoms rather than in combination with other atoms because they are extremely unreactive. _____

9. Scientists have prepared compounds for which four noble gases?

_____

Match each Group 0 gas with its uses.

_____ **10.** helium   **a.** inert atmospheres

_____ **11.** neon   **b.** artificial atmospheres

_____ **12.** argon   **c.** weather balloons

_____ **13.** krypton   **d.** neon signs

_____ **14.** xenon

25 HYDROCARBON COMPOUNDS

SECTION 25.1 HYDROCARBONS (pages 743–751)

This section describes the bonding in hydrocarbons and distinguishes between straight-chain and branched-chain alkanes.

▶ Organic Chemistry and Hydrocarbons (pages 743–745)

1. What is organic chemistry? _____

2. Organic compounds that contain only carbon and hydrogen are called

   _____ .

3. Is the following sentence true or false? Alkanes contain only single covalent

   bonds. _____

4. What is the simplest alkane? _____

5. Circle the letter of each statement that is true about carbon's ability to form bonds.

   a. Carbon atoms have four valence electrons.

   b. Carbon atoms always form three covalent bonds.

   c. Carbon atoms can form stable bonds with each other.

▶ Straight-Chain Alkanes (pages 745–747)

6. What are straight-chain alkanes? _____

   _____

   _____

   _____

7. The names of all alkanes end with the suffix _____ .

Match the name of the straight-chain alkane with the number of carbon atoms it contains.

_____ **8.** nonane   **a.** 3

_____ **9.** propane   **b.** 4

_____ **10.** heptane   **c.** 7

_____ **11.** butane   **d.** 9

12. The straight-chain alkanes are a(n) _____ because there
    is an incremental change of —CH$_2$— from one compound in the series to the next.

CHAPTER 25, Hydrocarbon Compounds *(continued)*

13. Circle the letter of each condensed structural formula for pentane.

   a. C_5H_{12}

   b. $CH_3CH_2CH_2CH_2CH_3$

   c. $CH_3(CH_2)_3CH_3$

   d. $C — C — C — C — C$

14. The _____ system names organic compounds according to their structure.

▶ Branched-Chain Alkanes (pages 748–751)

15. Is the following sentence true or false? Hydrogen atoms are the only atoms that can bond to the carbon atoms in a hydrocarbon. _____

16. A(n) _____ is an atom or group of atoms that replaces hydrogen in a hydrocarbon.

17. Alkyl groups are named by removing the *-ane* ending of the parent hydrocarbon and adding _____ to indicate that one _____ has been removed.

18. What is a branched-chain alkane? _____

19. Circle the letter of the correct IUPAC name for the molecule below.

$$CH_3—\overset{\overset{\displaystyle CH_3}{|}}{\underset{\underset{\displaystyle CH_3}{|}}{C}}—CH_2—\overset{\overset{\displaystyle CH_3}{|}}{CH}—CH_3$$

   a. 2,2,4-triethylpentane

   b. 3-methylpentane

   c. 2,2,4-trimethylpentane

20. Draw a condensed structural formula for 2-methylhexane.

▶ Properties of Alkanes (page 751)

21. Why are hydrocarbon molecules such as alkanes nonpolar? _____

   _____

   _____

22. Hydrocarbons and other nonpolar molecules are not attracted to

   _____ .

Reading Skill Practice

A flowchart can help you to remember the order in which events occur. On a separate sheet of paper, create a flowchart that describes the steps for naming branched-chain alkanes using the IUPAC system. This process is explained on pages 748–749.

SECTION 25.2 UNSATURATED HYDROCARBONS (pages 752–753)

This section explains the difference between unsaturated and saturated hydrocarbons. It also describes the difference between the structures of alkenes and alkynes.

▶ **Alkenes** (page 752)

1. What is an alkene?

   _____

2. Organic compounds that contain fewer than the maximum number of hydrogens in their structures are called _____ compounds.

3. Which family of hydrocarbons are always saturated compounds?

   _____

4. Circle the letter of the correct name for the alkene shown below.

   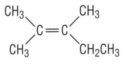

   a. 2,3-dimethyl-3-pentene   **c.** 2,3-dimethyl-2-pentene

   b. 2-methyl-3-methyl-2-pentene   **d.** 3-ethyl-2-methyl-2-butene

5. Is the following sentence true or false? Rotation can occur around a carbon–carbon double bond. _____

▶ **Alkynes** (page 753)

6. Hydrocarbons that contain one or more _____ covalent bonds between carbons are called alkynes.

7. _____ is the simplest alkyne, and is also known by the common name _____ .

CHAPTER 25, Hydrocarbon Compounds *(continued)*

8. What are the major attractive forces between alkane, alkene, or alkyne molecules? What physical properties can be explained by these forces?

_____

_____

9. Complete the table below with the names of the indicated alkanes, alkenes, and alkynes. For the alkenes and alkynes, assume that the multiple bond occurs between the first two carbons.

Number of Carbons	Alkane	Alkene	Alkyne
C_6			
C_7			
C_8			

10. Is the following sentence true or false? The angle between the carbon atoms in a carbon–carbon triple bond is 120°. _____

SECTION 25.3 ISOMERISM (pages 754–757)

This section explains how to distinguish among structural, geometric, and stereoisomers. It also describes how to identify the asymmetric carbon or carbons in stereoisomers.

▶ Structural Isomers (page 754)

1. What are structural isomers?

_____

_____

2. Is the following sentence true or false? Structural isomers have the same physical properties. _____

3. How many structural isomers are there for C_4H_{10}? _____

4. Name the structural isomers of C_4H_{10}. _____

5. In general, what determines which structural isomer will have the lowest boiling point? _____

_____

© Prentice-Hall, Inc.

▶ Geometric Isomers (pages 754–755)

6. Molecules that differ only in the spatial configuration of their substituted

groups are called _____ isomers.

7. What two things need to be present for the type of isomerism described in Question 6 to occur?

a. _____

b. _____

8. What are the names of the molecules represented by the ball-and-stick models below?

_____   _____

▶ Stereoisomers (pages 755–756)

9. _____ objects will produce a reflection that is indistinguishable from the original.

10. Mirror images that cannot be placed on top of each other to form a matching

pair are called _____ .

11. What is an asymmetric carbon?

_____

12. Is the following sentence true or false? Molecules that have an asymmetric

carbon have handedness. _____

13. Look at Figure 25.12 on page 755. Why are these two molecules stereoisomers?

_____

_____

14. Circle the two asymmetrical carbons in the structure shown below.

$$CH_3 - CH_2 - CH_2 - CH - CH - CH - CH_3$$
$$\qquad\qquad\qquad\quad\; | \qquad | \qquad |$$
$$\qquad\qquad\qquad\; CH_2 \quad CH_3 \quad CH_3$$
$$\qquad\qquad\qquad\quad |$$
$$\qquad\qquad\qquad\; CH_3$$

CHAPTER 25, Hydrocarbon Compounds *(continued)*

SECTION 25.4 HYDROCARBON RINGS (pages 759–761)

This section describes how to identify common cyclic ring structures. It also explains resonance in terms of the aromatic ring of benzene.

▶ **Cyclic Hydrocarbons** (page 759)

1. What is a cyclic hydrocarbon?

   _____

2. The most abundant cyclic hydrocarbons contain _____ or
   _____ carbons.

3. What are the names of the cyclic hydrocarbons represented below?

   a. _____   **b.** _____   **c.** _____   **d.** _____

4. Is the following sentence true or false? Cyclic hydrocarbons that contain only single carbon–carbon bonds are called cycloalkanes. _____

5. Circle the letter of each compound that is an aliphatic compound.

   a. cycloheptane

   b. butane

   c. acetylene

   d. 2-methylpropane

▶ **Aromatic Hydrocarbons** (pages 759–761)

6. _____ are a special group of unsaturated cyclic hydrocarbons.

7. Why were the arenes originally called aromatic compounds?

   _____

8. The simplest arene is _____ , which has a chemical formula of C_6H_6.

9. Is the following sentence true or false? Any substance that has carbon–carbon bonding like that of benzene is called an aromatic compound. _____

10. What does it mean to say that benzene exhibits resonance?

_____

11. Molecules that exhibit resonance are more _____ than similar molecules.

12. When _____ is a substituent on an alkane, it is called a phenyl group.

13. What is the chemical formula for a phenyl group? _____

14. Circle the letter of the name of the compound shown below.

CH₂CH₃   **a.** ethylhexene

           b. dimethylbenzene

           c. ethylbenzene

15. Derivatives of benzene that have _____ substituents are called disubstituted benzenes.

16. Why do disubstituted benzenes always have three structural isomers?

_____

Match the terms for naming a disubstituted benzene with the substituent positions they represent.

_____ **17.** *meta*   **a.** 1,2

_____ **18.** *ortho*   **b.** 1,3

_____ **19.** *para*   **c.** 1,4

20. What is another name for the dimethylbenzenes? _____

SECTION 25.5 HYDROCARBONS FROM THE EARTH (pages 762–765)

This section explains how to identify three important fossil fuels and describes their origins. It also names some products obtained from natural gas, petroleum, and coal.

▶ Natural Gas (pages 762–763)

1. What are fossil fuels?

_____

2. List the three factors needed to produce fossil fuels from organic residue.

a. _____   **b.** _____

c. _____

CHAPTER 25, Hydrocarbon Compounds *(continued)*

3. Petroleum and natural gas contain mostly _____ hydrocarbons.

4. Is the following sentence true or false? Natural gas and petroleum are often found together in dome-shaped geological formations. _____

5. What are the four main alkane components of natural gas?

_____

6. Which noble gas is found in natural gas? _____

7. Fill in the missing reactants and products in the equation for the combustion of methane.

$CH_4(g)$ + 2 _____ (g) ⟶ _____ (g) + 2 _____ (g) + heat

8. Propane and butane are sold in _____ form to be used

as _____ fuels.

9. _____ combustion of a hydrocarbon produces a blue flame;

_____ combustion produces a yellow flame.

10. What toxic gas is formed during incomplete combustion of a hydrocarbon?

_____

▶ Petroleum (pages 763–764)

11. The first oil well was drilled in _____ in the late 1850s.

12. Is the following sentence true or false? Crude oil is commercially useful

without refining. _____

13. How is crude oil refined?

_____

14. Circle the letter of the distillation fraction that represents the highest percent of crude oil.

a. natural gas

b. gasoline

c. kerosene

d. lubricating oil

15. Using a catalyst and heat to break hydrocarbons down into smaller molecules

is called _____ .

16. Complete the table below about four fractions obtained from crude oil. Indicate where each fraction will be collected from the fractionating column shown at the right.

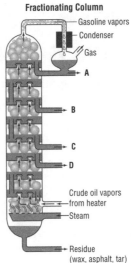

Fractionating Column

Fraction	Composition of Carbon Chains	Where in Column?
Fuel oil		
Gasoline		
Lubricating oil		

▶ **Coal** (pages 764–765)

17. _____ is the intermediate material that is the first stage in coal formation.

18. Name the three types of coal and the carbon content of each.

a. _____

b. _____

c. _____

19. Is the following sentence true or false? Coal mines in North America are usually at least a kilometer below Earth's surface. _____

20. Coal consists primarily of _____ compounds of extremely high molar mass.

21. Aromatic compounds produce more _____ when burned than do _____ fuels.

22. What major air pollutants are produced by burning coal that contains sulfur?

_____

23. List four products that can be obtained by distilling coal.

a. _____   c. _____

b. _____   d. _____

24. Which of these products can be distilled further?

_____

CHAPTER 25, Hydrocarbon Compounds (continued)

MathWise

GUIDED PRACTICE PROBLEM 4 (page 750)

4. Name these compounds according to the IUPAC system.

a. CH_3—CH_2—CH—CH_3
    |
    CH_3

b. CH_2—CH_2—CH—CH_2—CH_3
    | |
    CH_3 CH_2
              |
              CH_3

Use the steps on pages 748–749 to name each compound.

Step 1. How long is the longest string of carbon atoms? What is the name of the parent hydrocarbon structure?

a. _____   **b.** _____

Step 2. From which side will you number the carbon chain? Why?

a. _____

b. _____

Step 3. What are the names and positions of the substituents?

a. _____   **b.** _____

Step 4. Explain why neither name will contain a prefix.

a. _____

Step 5. Does the name contain any commas or hyphens?

a. _____

b. _____

Step 6. What is the complete name of each compound?

a. _____   **b.** _____

EXTRA PRACTICE PROBLEM (similar to Practice Problem 14, page 756)

14. Circle the symmetric carbon, if there is one, in each of these structures.

a. CH_3—CH—CH—CH_3
         | |
         CH_3 CH_3

b. CH_3—CH—CH_2—CH_2
              | |
              CH_2 CH_3
              |
              CH_3

© Prentice-Hall, Inc.

26 FUNCTIONAL GROUPS AND ORGANIC REACTIONS

SECTION 26.1 INTRODUCTION TO FUNCTIONAL GROUPS (pages 773–777)

This section defines a functional group and gives several examples. It also describes halocarbons and the substitution reactions they undergo.

▶ Functional Groups (pages 773–774)

1. Is the following sentence true or false? The saturated hydrocarbon skeletons of organic molecules are chemically reactive. _____

2. What is a functional group? _____

_____

Use Table 26.1 on page 774 to answer questions 3 and 4.

3. Name the functional group for each compound structure.

   a. $R-O-R$ _____   **b.** $R-OH$ _____   **c.** $R-NH_2$ _____

4. Name two compound types that have a carbonyl group as a functional group.

   a. _____   **b.** _____

▶ Halogen Substituents (pages 774–776)

5. What are halocarbons? _____

_____

6. Give the IUPAC and common names for the following halocarbons.

   a. $CH_3-CH_2-CH_2-Br$ _____

   b. $\begin{array}{c} H \\ H \end{array}\!\!>\!\!C=C\!\!<\!\!\begin{array}{c} I \\ H \end{array}$ _____

7. A halogen attached to a carbon of an aliphatic chain produces a halocarbon called a(n) _____ .

Match the prefix used in naming alkyl groups with its description.

   a. *iso-*   **b.** *sec-*   **c.** *tert-*

_____ 8. The carbon joining this alkyl group to another group is bonded to three other carbons.

_____ 9. The carbon joining this alkyl group to another group is bonded to two other carbons.

_____ 10. The carbon joining this alkyl group to another group is bonded to one other carbon.

CHAPTER 26, Functional Groups and Organic Reactions *(continued)*

11. What is an aryl halide? _____

_____

▶ Substitution Reactions *(pages 776–777)*

12. Why do reactions involving organic compounds often proceed more slowly than those involving inorganic molecules and ions?

_____

13. Is the following sentence true or false? The products of organic reactions are often a complex mixture of compounds. _____

14. Organic reactions that involve the replacement of one atom or group of atoms with another atom or group of atoms are called _____ reactions.

15. Label the compounds in this generalized equation. (X stands for a halogen.)

$$R\!-\!H \quad + \quad X_2 \quad \longrightarrow \quad R\!-\!X \quad + \quad HX$$

_____ _____ _____ _____

16. Hydroxide ions from sodium or potassium hydroxide can displace most

halogens on carbon chains to produce a(n) _____ .

SECTION 26.2 ALCOHOLS AND ETHERS *(pages 778–784)*

This section describes the structures and naming of alcohols and ethers, as well as comparing their properties. It also defines and gives examples of addition reactions.

▶ Alcohols *(pages 778–779)*

1. What are alcohols?

_____

2. The functional group in an alcohol is called a(n) _____ group.

Match each structural category of aliphatic alcohols with its description.

_____ **3.** primary alcohol   **a.** three R groups attached to C — OH

_____ **4.** secondary alcohol   **b.** one R group attached to C — OH

_____ **5.** tertiary alcohol   **c.** two R groups attached to C — OH

6. Circle the letter of the IUPAC ending used for an alcohol with two — OH substitutions.

   a. *-ol*   **b.** *-tetrol*   **c.** *-triol*   **d.** *-diol*

7. _____ is the common name for alcohols with more than one
— OH substituent.

8. Write the IUPAC name and the common name for each alcohol shown.

   a. CH_3 — CH_3 — OH   _____

               OH
               |
   b. CH_3 — CH — CH_3 _____

   c. CH_2 — CH — CH_2 _____
        | | |
       OH   OH   OH

▶ Properties of Alcohols (pages 779–781)

9. Is the following sentence true or false? Alcohols cannot form intermolecular

    hydrogen bonds. _____

10. What are the two parts of an alcohol molecule?

    _____

11. Why are alcohols with four or more carbons not soluble in water?

    _____

    _____

12. Name two uses for isopropyl alcohol.

      a. _____

      b. _____

13. Which alcohol is used in many antifreezes? _____

14. The action of yeast or bacteria on sugars to produce ethanol is called

    _____ .

15. How is ethanol denatured?

    _____

▶ Addition Reactions (pages 781–783)

16. Adding new functional groups at the double or triple bond of an alkene or

    alkyne is called a(n) _____ reaction.

17. Is the following sentence true or false? Adding a hydrogen halide to an alkene

    results in a disubstituted halocarbon. _____

CHAPTER 26, Functional Groups and Organic Reactions (continued)

18. Look at the reaction between ethene and water:

$$\underset{H}{\overset{H}{\diagdown}}C=C\underset{H}{\overset{H}{\diagup}} \ + \ H-OH \ \xrightarrow[100\,°C]{H^+}$$

a. Draw the structure of the product.

_____

b. What type of compound is the product? _____

c. What is this type of addition reaction called? _____

d. What is the role of the hydrogen ions? _____

19. What type of reaction is used to manufacture margarine from unsaturated vegetable oils? _____

20. Which hydrocarbon resists addition reactions? _____

▶ Ethers (pages 783–784)

21. An ether is a compound in which _____ is bonded to two carbon groups.

22. How are ethers named? _____

_____

23. Circle the letter of each symmetrical ether.

a. ethylmethyl ether

c. diphenyl ether

b. diethyl ether

d. methylphenyl ether

24. Is the following sentence true or false? Ethers have higher boiling points than alcohols of comparable molar mass. _____

Reading Skill Practice

By looking carefully at photographs and diagrams in your textbook, you can better understand what you have read. Look carefully at Figure 26.9 on page 782. What important idea does this drawing communicate? Do your work on a separate sheet of paper.

SECTION 26.3 CARBONYL COMPOUNDS (pages 785–794)

This section explains how to distinguish among the carbonyl groups of aldehydes, ketones, carboxylic acids, and esters. It also describes the reactions of compounds that contain the carbonyl group.

▶ **Aldehydes and Ketones** (pages 785–787)

1. A _____ consists of a carbon joined by a double bond to an oxygen atom.

2. What is the difference between an aldehyde and a ketone? _____

_____

_____

3. What ending is used in the IUPAC system to indicate an aldehyde? a ketone?

_____

4. Circle the letter of each statement that is true about aldehydes and ketones.

   a. In an aldehyde or ketone sample, the molecules cannot form intermolecular hydrogen bonds.

   b. The molecules in an aldehyde or ketone sample do not attract each other through polar–polar interactions.

   c. Most aldehydes and ketones are gases at room temperature.

   d. Aldehydes and ketones can form weak hydrogen bonds with water.

Match the aldehyde or ketone with its use.

_____	**5.** methanal	**a.** almond flavoring
_____	**6.** propanone	**b.** preservative
_____	**7.** benzaldehyde	**c.** oil of cinnamon
_____	**8.** 3-phenyl-2-propenal	**d.** solvent

9. Aromatic aldehydes are often used as _____ agents.

▶ **Carboxylic Acids** (pages 788–789)

10. What is a carboxyl group?

_____

11. Is the following sentence true or false? Carboxylic acids are weak acids. _____

12. What ending is used under the IUPAC system to designate a carboxylic acid?

_____

13. Carboxylic acids with three or more carbons in a straight chain are also known

as _____ acids.

© Prentice-Hall, Inc.

CHAPTER 26, Functional Groups and Organic Reactions *(continued)*

14. Complete the table about saturated aliphatic carboxylic acids.

IUPAC Name	Common Name	Carbon Atoms	Formula
		4	$CH_3(CH_2)_2COOH$
Octanoic acid			$CH_3(CH_2)_6COOH$
	Acetic acid	2	
Octadecanoic acid	Stearic acid		

15. What form do all aromatic carboxylic acids have at room temperature?

_____

_____

▶ Esters (pages 789–791)

16. An ester is a derivative of a _____ that has an — OR substituted for the — OH.

17. Write the general formula for an ester. _____

18. What two products are formed when an ester is hydrolyzed in the presence of a strong acid or base?

_____

_____

▶ Oxidation-Reduction Reactions (pages 791–794)

19. Are triple carbon–carbon bonds more or less oxidized than double and single

carbon–carbon bonds? _____

20. What is a dehydrogenation reaction? _____

_____

21. Circle the letter of the compound that is the final product of methane oxidation.

    a. methanol   **c.** methanal

    b. formic acid   **d.** carbon dioxide

22. Primary alcohols are oxidized to form _____ , but secondary

alcohols form _____ when oxidized.

23. Why are tertiary alcohols resistant to oxidation? _____

_____

24. Is the following sentence true or false? The oxidation of organic compounds

    is exothermic. _____

25. What property of aldehydes do Fehling's test and Benedict's test take
    advantage of? What color is the precipitate that forms?

    _____

SECTION 26.4 POLYMERIZATION (pages 795–800)

This section defines polymers and monomers. It also names and describes the uses of some important addition and condensation polymers.

▶ **Addition Polymers (pages 795–797)**

1. What are polymers? _____

   _____

2. Is the following sentence true or false? Polymers can only contain one type of

   monomer. _____

3. Most polymerization reactions require a _____ .

4. Complete the table by naming each polymer.

Polymer	Structure
	$H \left[CH_2 - CH_2 \right]_x H$
	$\left[CH_2 - \underset{\underset{CH_3}{\vert}}{CH} \right]_x$
	$\left[CH_2 - \underset{\underset{Cl}{\vert}}{CH} \right]_x$
	$\left[CF_2 - CF_2 \right]_x$

Match the polymer with its use.

_____ **5.** polyethylene   **a.** foam coffee cups

_____ **6.** polystyrene   **b.** rubber tubing

_____ **7.** polytetrafluoroethene   **c.** nonstick cookware

_____ **8.** polyisoprene   **d.** plastic wrap

_____ **9.** polyvinyl chloride   **e.** plumbing pipes

CHAPTER 26, Functional Groups and Organic Reactions (continued)

▶ Condensation Polymers (pages 798–800)

10. How is a polyester formed? _____

_____

11. For condensation polymerization to occur, each monomer molecule must

have _____ functional groups.

12. Name the two monomer molecules that are joined to form the polyester PET.

_____

13. Garments made from PET fibers are _____ resistant.

14. Is the following sentence true or false? The polymer produced by the

condensation of a carboxylic acid and an amine is called an amide. _____

15. What common group of synthetic materials is made up by polyamides?

_____

16. _____ are an important group of naturally occurring

polyamides made from monomers called _____ .

Match each common polymer to its structural representation.

_____ **17.**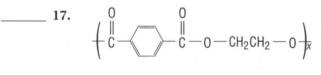

a. Kevlar
b. Nomex
c. nylon
d. PET

_____ **18.**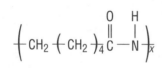

_____ **19.**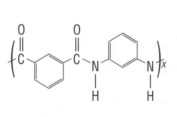

_____ **20.**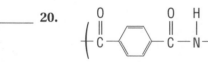

Name _____ Date _____ Class _____

THE CHEMISTRY OF LIFE

SECTION 27.1 A STRATEGY FOR LIFE (pages 809–811)

This section describes the structure of a typical eukaryotic cell. It also explains the relationship between photosynthesis and all life on Earth.

▶ The Structure of Cells (pages 809–810)

1. What are the two major types of cell design?

   a. _____   b. _____

2. Which of the two cell types are found in humans?

   _____

3. Fill in the missing labels for structures in the drawing of a eukaryotic cell.

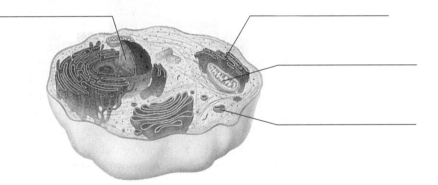

4. Is the following sentence true or false? Both cell types are surrounded by a cell membrane that acts as a selective barrier to the passage of chemicals into or out of the cell. _____

5. Only eukaryotic cells contain membrane-enclosed _____ in which specialized functions of the cell occur.

Match the organelle to its function.

_____ 6. mitochondrion   **a.** manufacture of proteins

_____ 7. nucleus   **b.** cell reproduction

_____ 8. lysosome   **c.** energy production

_____ 9. endoplasmic reticulum **d.** digestion

© Prentice-Hall, Inc.

CHAPTER 27, The Chemistry of Life *(continued)*

▶ Energy and Carbon Cycle (pages 810–811)

10. What is the source of all energy for life on Earth? _____

11. Circle the letter of the process by which organisms capture and use this energy to make food.

    a. oxidation   **b.** photosynthesis   **c.** digestion   **d.** respiration

12. How do plants use the energy they obtain from sunlight?

    _____

13. Explain how animals obtain the energy they need.

    _____

    _____

14. What are the products of the oxidation of glucose?

    _____

15. Is the following sentence true or false? The destruction of forests and pollution of the oceans has no effect on the survival of animal life.

    _____

SECTION 27.2   CARBOHYDRATES (pages 812–814)

This section describes the important structural characteristics of monosaccharides, disaccharides, and polysaccharides. It also lists the sources and uses for a number of important carbohydrates.

▶ Monosaccharides (pages 812–813)

1. Carbohydrates are made from aldehydes and ketones that contain many

   _____ groups.

2. Name the three elements present in carbohydrates.

   a. _____   **b.** _____   **c.** _____

3. What is the general formula for a carbohydrate? _____

4. What is another name for simple sugars? _____

5. Circle the letter of each simple sugar.

    a. glucose   **b.** sucrose   **c.** fructose   **d.** starch

▶ Disaccharides and Polysaccharides (pages 813-814)

6. Sugars formed by linking two monosaccharides are called _____ .

© Prentice-Hall, Inc.

7. What compound is lost in the reaction that links two monosaccharides?

_____

8. Is the following sentence true or false? Sucrose, or table sugar, is formed by the polymerization of two glucose molecules. _____

9. What are polysaccharides? _____

_____

10. Complete the following table about polysaccharides.

Polysaccharide	Source	Function
starch		
		energy storage
	plants	

SECTION 27.3 AMINO ACIDS AND THEIR POLYMERS (pages 815–819)

This section explains how to write a general formula for an amino acid and describes the bonding between amino acids. It also describes the effect of enzymes on biochemical reactions.

▶ Amino Acids (page 815)

1. A family of plants called legumes reduce atmospheric nitrogen to ammonia in a process called _____ .

2. What is an amino acid? How many amino acids are found in living organisms?

_____

_____

_____

3. What determines the physical and chemical properties of an amino acid?

_____

Match the amino acid to its abbreviation.

_____ **4.** Glutamine   **a.** Ile

_____ **5.** Isoleucine   **b.** Trp

_____ **6.** Methionine   **c.** Pro

_____ **7.** Proline   **d.** Gln

_____ **8.** Tryptophan   **e.** Met

CHAPTER 27, The Chemistry of Life *(continued)*

▶ Peptides *(page 816)*

9. What is a peptide?

_____

_____

10. The bond between amino acids is called a(n) _____ bond.

11. Is the following sentence true or false? The bond between amino acids always involves the side chains. _____

12. The formula for peptides is written so that the free _____ group is on the left end and the free _____ group is on the right end.

13. Is the following sentence true or false? The order of the amino acids in a peptide can be reversed and still represent the same peptide. _____

▶ Proteins *(pages 816–817)*

14. A(n) _____ contains more than ten amino acids, but a(n) _____ has more than 100 amino acids.

15. The chemical and physiological properties of a protein are determined by its _____ sequence.

16. Name each type of structure that can be formed by folding long peptide chains.

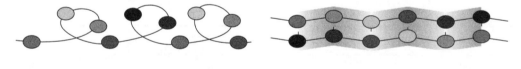

_____   _____

17. What types of bonds maintain the three-dimensional shape of a folded protein? _____

_____

18. Is the following sentence true or false? A single protein can be made from separate polypeptide chains, held together by bonds between side-chain groups. _____

▶ Enzymes *(pages 818–819)*

19. What are enzymes?

_____

20. What three properties of a catalyst do enzymes have?

a. _____

b. _____

c. _____

21. Is the following sentence true or false? Because an active site fits a specific substrate, each enzyme catalyzes only one chemical reaction.

_____

22. What is the enzyme molecule joined to its substrate molecule called?

_____

Match the enzyme to its substrate.

_____ **23.** urease   **a.** carbonic acid

_____ **24.** carbonic anhydrase   **b.** hydrogen peroxide

_____ **25.** catalase   **c.** urea

26. What is a coenzyme? Give two examples. _____

_____

SECTION 27.4 LIPIDS (pages 821–823)

This section characterizes the molecular structure of triglycerides, phospholipids, and waxes. It also describes the functions of phospholipids and proteins in cell membranes.

▶ Triglycerides (pages 821–822)

1. Fats provide an efficient means of _____ for your body.

2. What are lipids? _____

3. Triglycerides are triesters of one _____ molecule and three

_____ molecules.

4. Complete the following table about two types of triglycerides.

Triglyceride Type	State at Room Temperature	Primary Source
fats		
		plants

5. Circle the letter of the process used to make soap.

a. hydrogenation   c. denaturation

b. saponification   d. polymerization

CHAPTER 27, The Chemistry of Life *(continued)*

▶ Phospholipids (pages 822–823)

6. What is the molecular structure of a phospholipid?

_____

7. How does the chemical nature of a phospholipid affect its solubility?

_____

_____

8. When phospholipids are added to water, they spontaneously form a lipid

_____ , with the hydrophobic tails located in the

_____ .

9. How does a cell membrane accomplish selective absorption?

_____

_____

_____

▶ Waxes (page 823)

10. What is the molecular structure of waxes?

_____

11. Is the following sentence true or false? Waxes are liquid at room temperature.

_____

12. Name two functions of waxes in plants.

_____

SECTION 27.5 NUCLEIC ACIDS (pages 824–831)

This section describes the structural components of nucleotides and nucleic acids, including DNA, and gives simple examples of genetic mutations. It also explains what is meant by recombinant DNA technology.

▶ DNA and RNA (pages 824–826)

1. What are the functions of the two types of nucleic acids?

_____

_____

2. The monomers that make up nucleic acids are called _____ .

© Prentice-Hall, Inc.

3. Name the three parts of a nucleotide.

a. _____ b. _____ c. _____

4. What nitrogen bases are found in DNA? in RNA?

_____

_____

5. DNA molecules consist of two chains of nucleotides that are bound together

into a double _____ .

6. Name the complementary base pairs found in DNA.

a. _____ b. _____

▶ The Genetic Code (pages 826–827)

7. What is a gene?

_____

8. How many nucleotides are needed to code for one amino acid? _____

9. The _____ is the arrangement of code words in DNA that provides the information to make specific proteins.

10. Is the following sentence true or false? Each amino acid has only one DNA

code word. _____

11. Use Table 27.2 on page 827. Which amino acids are coded in the nucleotide sequence TACAGCCTCGACAAG?

_____

12. Circle the letter of each code word that represents a termination signal.

a. ATT   b. AAC   c. ATC   d. AAT

▶ Gene Mutations (pages 828–829)

13. Circle the letter of each event that could cause a gene mutation.

a. substitution of one or more nucleotides

b. addition of one or more nucleotides

c. deletion of one or more nucleotides

14. What is the effect of mutations on the production of proteins?

_____

_____

_____

CHAPTER 27, The Chemistry of Life *(continued)*

15. Is the following sentence true or false? Diseases resulting from gene mutations are called inborn errors. _____

16. Name two diseases that are caused by mutations in the hemoglobin gene.

_____

▶ DNA Fingerprinting (pages 829–830)

17. DNA base sequences differ for everyone except _____ .

18. Complete the flowchart about DNA fingerprinting.

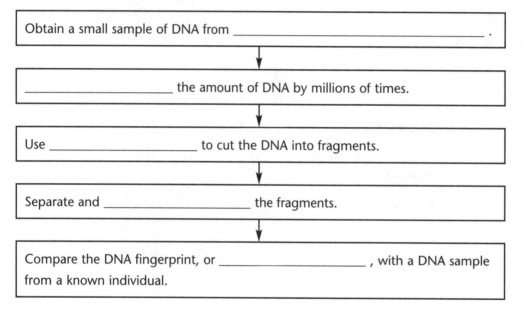

> Obtain a small sample of DNA from _____ .
>
> ↓
>
> _____ the amount of DNA by millions of times.
>
> ↓
>
> Use _____ to cut the DNA into fragments.
>
> ↓
>
> Separate and _____ the fragments.
>
> ↓
>
> Compare the DNA fingerprint, or _____ , with a DNA sample from a known individual.

19. What are the disadvantages of DNA fingerprinting in criminal cases?

_____

_____

▶ Recombinant DNA Technology (pages 830–831)

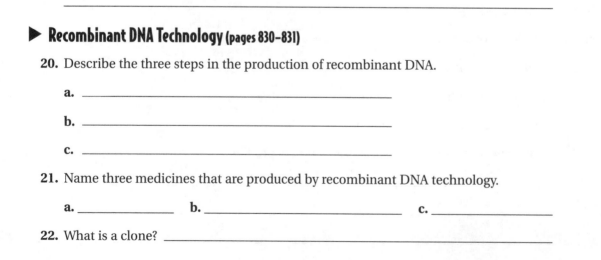

20. Describe the three steps in the production of recombinant DNA.

a. _____

b. _____

c. _____

21. Name three medicines that are produced by recombinant DNA technology.

a. _____ b. _____ c. _____

22. What is a clone? _____

Name _____ Date _____ Class _____

SECTION 27.6 METABOLISM (pages 832–834)

This section describes the role of ATP in energy production and energy use in the cell. It also defines metabolism and explains the relationship between catabolism and anabolism.

▶ ATP (pages 832–833)

1. What is ATP and what is its function?

_____

2. Energy is captured when a _____ group is added to adenosine diphosphate (ADP).

3. a. How much energy is stored when one mole of ATP is produced? _____

   b. How much energy is released when one mole of ATP is hydrolyzed back to ADP? _____

4. ATP is important because it occupies an _____ position beween higher-energy _____ reactions and other celluar processes.

▶ Catabolism (pages 833–834)

5. The entire set of all chemical reactions that are carried out in a living organism is called _____ .

6. What is catabolism? _____

_____

7. Circle the letter of each product of catabolism.

   a. heat   c. complex biological molecules

   b. ATP   d. building blocks for new compounds

8. One of the most important catabolic processes is the complete oxidation of _____ to form _____ and water.

9. How much energy is released by the complete combustion of one mole of glucose? _____

10. How many moles of ATP are produced by the complete oxidation of one mole of glucose? _____

11. Is the following sentence true or false? All the reactions involved in the complete oxidation of glucose are shown in Figure 27.26.

_____

© Prentice-Hall, Inc.

CHAPTER 27, The Chemistry of Life *(continued)*

12. Use Figure 27.26 to fill in the names of the carbon-containing molecules and ions represented.

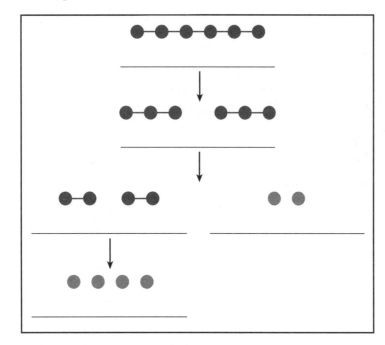

▶ **Anabolism** (page 834)

13. Anabolic reactions are _____ reactions that produce more-complex biological molecules.

14. Catabolic reactions _____ energy, whereas anabolic

    reactions _____ energy.

15. Look at Figure 27.27. Explain why all the terms that appear in the yellow ovals also appear in the blue ovals.

    _____

    _____

    _____

📖 Reading Skill Practice

By looking carefully at photographs and drawings in your textbook, you can better understand what you have read. Look carefully at Figure 27.25 on page 833. What important idea does this drawing communicate? Do your work on a separate sheet of paper.

28 NUCLEAR CHEMISTRY

SECTION 28.1 NUCLEAR RADIATION (pages 841–844)

This section describes the nature of radioactivity and the process of radioactive decay. It characterizes alpha, beta, and gamma radiation in terms of composition and penetrating power.

▶ Radioactivity (pages 841–842)

1. An isotope that has an unstable nucleus is called a(n) _____ .

2. Complete the table below to show basic differences between chemical and nuclear reactions.

Type of Reaction	Is Nucleus of Atom Changed?	Is Reaction Affected by Temperature, Pressure, or Catalysts?
Chemical		
Nuclear		

3. Look at Figure 28.1 on page 841. Which French chemist noticed that uranium salts could fog photographic plates, even without being exposed to sunlight?

   _____

4. What name did Marie Curie give to the process by which materials give off rays capable of fogging photographic plates? _____

5. Complete the flowchart below, which describes the radioactive decay process.

   The presence of too many or too few _____ relative to protons leads to an unstable nucleus.

   ↓

   At some point in time, an unstable nucleus will undergo a reaction and lose energy by emitting _____ .

   ↓

   During the process of radioactive decay, an _____ radioisotope of one element is transformed eventually into a _____ isotope of a different element.

CHAPTER 28, Nuclear Chemistry *(continued)*

▶ Types of Radiation (pages 842–844)

6. Complete the following table showing some characteristics of the main types of radiation commonly emitted during radioactive decay.

Type			
Consists of	2 protons and 2 neutrons	electron (or positron)	high-energy electromagnetic radiation
Mass (amu)			
Penetrating power (low, moderate, or high)			
Minimum shielding			

7. Look at Figure 28.3 on page 843. It shows the alpha decay of uranium-238 to thorium-234.

  a. What is the change in atomic number after the alpha decay?

  _____

  b. What is the change in mass number after the alpha decay?

  _____

8. When are radioisotopes that emit alpha particles dangerous to soft tissues?

  _____

9. Look at Figure 28.4 on page 843. This diagram shows the beta decay of carbon-14 to nitrogen-14.

  a. What is the change in atomic number after the beta decay?

  _____

  b. Which quantity changes in beta decay, the mass number or the charge of

  the nucleus? _____

10. Explain how gamma radiation is similar to visible light, and how it is different.

  Similar: _____

  Different: _____

11. When are gamma rays emitted? _____

  _____

12. Is the following sentence true or false? Gamma rays have no mass and no

electrical charge. _____

13. Look at the diagram below. Below each material indicate with a checkmark which type of radiation—alpha, beta, or gamma—can be stopped by each material.

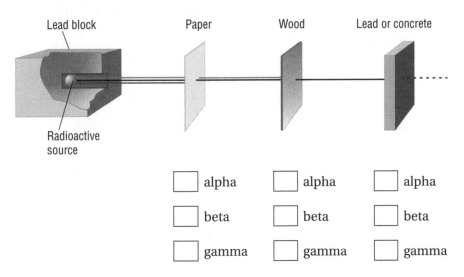

	alpha		alpha		alpha
	beta		beta		beta
	gamma		gamma		gamma

14. Is the following sentence true or false? X-rays are emitted during radioactive

decay. _____

SECTION 28.2 NUCLEAR TRANSFORMATIONS (pages 845–851)

This section relates nuclear stability and decay to the ratio of neutrons to protons. It explains the use of half-life to measure the lifetime of unstable nuclei and gives examples of transmutations.

▶ Nuclear Stability and Decay (pages 845–846)

1. Of about 1500 different nuclei that are known to exist, about what portion are stable?

   a. 1 of 10   **b.** 1 of 6   **c.** 1 of 3   **d.** 1 of 2

2. Stable nuclei have roughly _____ numbers of neutrons and protons.

3. Look at Figure 28.6 on page 845. How does the ratio of neutrons to protons for the stable nuclei change as atomic number increases from 1 to 82?

_____

4. A positron has the mass of a(n) _____ but its charge is

_____ .

CHAPTER 28, Nuclear Chemistry *(continued)*

5. Complete the table below showing changes in charge and number of neutrons and protons for different types of nuclear decay.

Reason Nucleus Is Unstable	Type of Decay	Change in Nuclear Charge	Change in Number of Protons and Neutrons
Too many neutrons	Beta particle		
Too many protons	Electron capture		
Too many protons	Positron (Beta particle)		
Too many protons and neutrons	Alpha particle		

▶ Half-Life (pages 847–850)

6. What is half-life? _____

_____

7. Look at Table 28.2 on page 847 to help you answer the following questions.

  a. What is the half-life in years of carbon-14? _____

  b. How many years old is an artifact that contains 50% of its original carbon-14? An artifact that contains 25% of its original carbon-14?

_____

8. The decay reaction below shows how a radioactive form of potassium found in many minerals decays into argon (gas).

  a. Fill in the missing mass number and atomic number for the argon isotope that results from the decay of potassium-40.

$$^{40}_{19}K + \ ^{0}_{-1}e \longrightarrow \ ^{\square}_{\square}Ar$$

  b. Look at Table 28.2 on page 847. What radiation is emitted when potassium-40 decays? _____

  c. What is the half-life of potassium-40? _____

  d. Which isotopes listed in Table 28.2 have a half-life similar to that of potassium-40? _____

© Prentice-Hall, Inc.

▶ **Transmutation Reactions** (pages 850–851)

9. The conversion of an atom of one element to an atom of another element is called _____ .

10. What are two ways transmutation can occur? _____

_____

11. Uranium-238 undergoes 14 transmutations before it reaches the stable isotope

_____ .

12. Is the following sentence true or false? All transuranium elements were synthesized in nuclear reactors and accelerators. _____

 Reading Skill Practice

By looking carefully at photographs and graphs in your textbook, you help yourself understand what you have read. Look carefully at Figure 28.7 on page 847. What important idea does this graph communicate? If you were to extend the curve indefinitely, would the percent of radio-isotope remaining ever cross 0%? Why or why not? Do your work on a separate sheet of paper.

SECTION 28.3 FISSION AND FUSION OF ATOMIC NUCLEI (pages 853–856)

This section describes nuclear fission and nuclear fusion. It discusses their potential as sources of energy, methods used to control them, and issues involved in containment of nuclear waste.

▶ **Nuclear Fission** (pages 853–855)

1. When certain heavy isotopes are bombarded with _____ , they split into smaller fragments.

2. Use the following labels to complete the diagram below: *fission, fission fragments,* and *neutrons/chain reaction.*

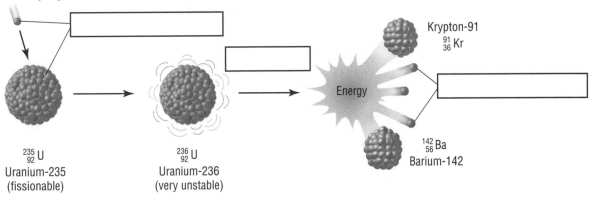

$^{235}_{92}$U
Uranium-235
(fissionable)

$^{236}_{92}$U
Uranium-236
(very unstable)

Energy

Krypton-91
$^{91}_{36}$Kr

$^{142}_{56}$Ba
Barium-142

© Prentice-Hall, Inc.

CHAPTER 28, Nuclear Chemistry *(continued)*

3. The uncontrolled fission of 1 kg of uranium-235 can release energy equal to

    _____ tons of dynamite.

4. Look at Figure 28.12 on page 854. This figure shows the basic components of a nuclear power reactor.

    a. What part of the reactor contains the nuclear fuel?

    _____

    b. What are the two parts of the reactor that control the fission reaction, one by reducing the speed of neutrons, the other by absorbing neutrons?

    _____

    c. What is the role of the coolant? _____

    _____

▶ Nuclear Waste (page 855)

5. Which parts of a nuclear reactor must be removed and replaced periodically?

    _____

6. Look at Figure 28.13 on page 855. Where are spent fuel rods stored in a typical nuclear power plant?

    _____

7. Circle the letter of each sentence that is true about nuclear waste.

    a. Spent fuel rods are considered high-level nuclear waste.

    b. All the highly radioactive fission products have very short half-lives.

    c. Assemblies of spent fuel rods may spend a decade or more in a holding pool.

    d. A decommissioned nuclear plant is contaminated with radioactive materials.

▶ Nuclear Fusion (page 856)

8. Look at Figure 28.14 on page 856. What happens to each pair of hydrogen nuclei during nuclear fusion?

    _____

9. What problem has prevented the practical use of nuclear fusion?

    _____

    _____

SECTION 28.4 RADIATION IN YOUR LIFE (pages 857–861)

This section explains three methods of detecting radiation and describes applications of radioisotopes in medicine and research.

▶ Detecting Radiation (page 857–859)

1. Why are beta particles called ionizing radiation? _____

_____

Look at the diagram of a Geiger counter to help you answer Questions 2, 3, and 4.

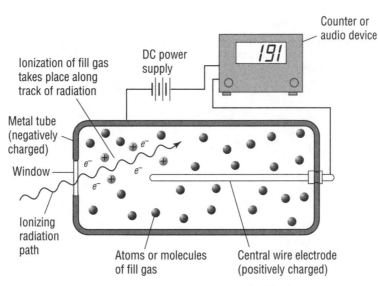

2. Draw in an arrow next to the central wire electrode to show the direction in which electron current flows when a beta particle enters the tube.

3. Is a radiation source that produces 191 clicks per second stronger or weaker

than a source that produces 191 clicks per minute? _____

4. A device that detects flashes of light after ionizing radiation strikes a specially

coated phosphor surface is called a _____ .

▶ Using Radiation (pages 859–861)

5. How is neutron activation analysis used?

_____

6. Look at Figure 28.18 on page 860. How is radioactive iodine-131 being used as

a diagnostic tool? _____

_____

7. Look at Figure 28.19 on page 861. When are cells most vulnerable to radiation?

_____

MathWise

GUIDED PRACTICE PROBLEM 4 (page 849)

4. Manganese-56 is a beta emitter with a half-life of 2.6 h. What is the mass of manganese-56 in a 1.0-mg sample of the isotope at the end of 10.4 h?

Analyze

Step 1. What are the known values?

_____

Step 2. How many half-lives have passed during the elapsed time?

$$\text{Number of half-lives} = \frac{\text{elapsed time}}{t_{1/2}} = \frac{\boxed{}}{2.6 \text{ h/half-life}} = \boxed{} \text{ half-lives}$$

Solve

Step 3. Multiply the initial mass by $\frac{1}{2}$ for each half-life.

1.0 mg × _____ = _____ mg Mn-56

Evaluate

Step 4. How do you know your answer is correct? _____

_____

EXTRA PRACTICE (similar to Practice Problem 4, page 849)

4. Iodine-126 is a beta emitter with a half-life of 13 days. What is the mass of iodine-126 in a 8.0-mg sample of the isotope at the end of 39 days?

GUIDED PRACTICE PROBLEM 5 (page 850)

5. A sample of thorium-234 has a half-life of 25 days. Will all the thorium undergo radioactive decay in 50 days? Explain.

Step 1. How many half-lives have passed in 50 days?

$$\frac{50 \text{ days}}{\boxed{}} = \boxed{} \text{ half-lives}$$

Step 2. What fraction of the thorium will remain after 50 days?

_____

Step 3. Will all the thorium decay in 50 days? Explain.

_____